Creating Meaningful Funeral *Experiences*

A Guide for Caregivers

REVISED EDITION

ALAN D. WOLFELT, PH.D.

Also by Alan D. Wolfelt, Ph.D.:

Funeral Home Customer Service A-Z: Creating Exceptional Experiences for Today's Families

The Journey Through Grief: Reflections on Healing

Healing the Bereaved Child: Grief Gardening, Growth Through Grief and Other Touchstones for Caregivers

Healing Your Grieving Heart: 100 Practical Ideas

Understanding Your Grief: Ten Essential Touchstones for Finding Hope and Healing Your Heart

Creating Meaningful Funeral Ceremonies: A Guide for Families

Companion Press is dedicated to the education and support of both the bereaved and bereavement caregivers. We believe that those who companion the bereaved by walking with them as they journey in grief have a wondrous opportunity: to help others embrace and grow through grief—and to lead fuller, more deeply-lived lives themselves because of this important ministry.
Companion Press is a division of the Center for Loss and Life Transition, located in Fort Collins, Colorado.

For ordering information, write or call:
Companion Press
a division of
The Center for Loss and Life Transition
3735 Broken Bow Road
Fort Collins, CO 80526
(970) 226-6050
www.centerforloss.com

Creating Meaningful Funeral *Experiences*

A Guide for Caregivers

REVISED EDITION

Alan D. Wolfelt, Ph.D.

Companion
PRESS
An imprint of the Center for Loss and Life Transition

Companion Press is an imprint of the Center for Loss and Life Transition,

3735 Broken Bow Road, Fort Collins, Colorado 80526.

Manufactured in the Unites States of America

16 15 14 13 12 11 5 4 3 2 1

ISBN: 978-1-879651-38-8

"Show me the manner in which a nation or a community cares for its dead and I will measure with mathematical exactness the tender mercies of its people, their respect for the law of the land, and their loyalty to high ideals."

– William Gladstone

Contents

Preface	1
Introduction	5
Part 1: Influences on the Deritualization of the Funeral	11
Part 2: Exploring the Purposes of Meaningful Funeral Ceremonies	19
Part 3: It's the Experience That Counts	31
Part 4: The Caregiver's Role in Creating Meaningful Funeral Ceremonies	43
Part 5: Practical Ideas for Creating Meaningful Funerals	57
Authentic Funeral Ceremonies: An Outline	89
A Final Word	94
Ten Freedoms for Planning Meaningful Funerals	95
Recommended Readings	97
About the Author	98

Preface

"(Ritual) is a pattern imposed on the mere flux of our feelings by reason and will, which renders pleasures less fugitive and griefs more endurable, which hands over to the power of wise custom the task (to which the individual and his moods are so inadequate) of being festive or sober, gay or reverent, when we choose to be, and not at the bidding of chance."
– C.S. Lewis

I have had the privilege of companioning thousands of mourners who have been willing to teach me about their grief journeys. I also have experienced how my own personal losses have changed my life forever. In these ways I have learned that meaningful funeral ceremonies are one of the most affirming means of helping our fellow human beings begin to embrace the pain of separation and loss after the death of someone loved.

Meaningful funeral ceremonies can and do make a significant difference in how grieving families channel their grief toward health and healing. During the funeral the community comes together and responds not only to the reality that someone has died, but also to the reality that those remaining will need support, compassion, love, hope, and understanding. More, an authentic funeral is often the beginning of the expression of grief. What happens at the funeral (and how it happens) greatly affects how the mourners go on to find meaning and purpose in their continued living.

Creating meaningful ceremonies when death impacts us can assist us with emotional, physical, and spiritual transformations. The death of someone we love often temporarily disconnects us from ourselves and the world around us. As we search for some sense of balance, we must make internal adaptations to our new outer reality: someone who has been physically present in our lives is gone. Participating in a meaningful funeral experience helps us begin to re-center ourselves, to make that painful but necessary transition from life before the death to life after the death.

Helen Keller provided us with a simple yet profound metaphor when she said, "The only way to get to the other side is to go through the door." Meaningful

Companioning the Bereaved

To "companion" the bereaved means to be an active participant in their healing. When you as a caregiver companion the bereaved, you allow yourself to learn from their unique experiences. You let the bereaved teach you instead of the other way around. You make the commitment to walk with them as they journey through grief.

funerals are doorways to healing for those who mourn. Some mourners, following the current North American trend away from funerals, are choosing never to enter the doorway. Many, unaware of the ways in which authentic funerals can help them, are blindly choosing doorways that lead nowhere. More families than ever before are using the words "direct cremation and no service." But a lucky few are led through the very special doorways that open onto the many paths to grief's reconciliation. You, the bereavement caregiver (whether you are a clergy person, funeral director, celebrant or grief counselor), have the opportunity to lead mourners through doorways that allow them to say "hello on the pathway to goodbye" through the use of meaningful funeral ceremonies.

Becoming an Educator on Meaningful Funerals

As a death educator and grief counselor, I wrote the first edition of Creating Meaningful Funeral Experiences in 1994 out of a deep concern that individuals, families and ultimately society as a whole would suffer if we did not reinvest ourselves in the funeral ritual. In 2003, I updated this book with an eye to the many signs of progress I had seen. The 2011 update of this book calls for industry leaders to become educators on meaningful funerals.

There is a vital need for those of us who recognize the value of meaningful funerals to serve as educators about that value. Why? Because many people, through no fault of their own, have not learned that "when words are inadequate, have ceremony." Instead, more people than we have ever witnessed before are questioning the very value of funerals. Many confuse efficiency with effectiveness and move away from befriending their grief by saying, "It will just be easier if…." They go on (unless we supportively teach them value) to eliminate elements of ceremony like visitations, music, symbols, readings, prayer, and sharing. The result fits with what T.S. Elliot observed: "You can have an experience and miss the meaning." This calls for all of us concerned about the future of meaningful funerals to gently, yet firmly, teach our fellow human beings about the tremendous importance of "getting off to a good start" in grief through well-planned ceremony.

While it is tempting to think that your job is to create a celebration or a party when it's requested, I urge you to pause for a moment and consider what's best for the families you serve. We are witnessing, and I suggest even colluding with, a powerful trend toward celebrations and parties and away from meaningful funeral experiences. According to a 2010 survey by Funeralwise.com, 48 percent of 1643 respondents said they would want a "celebration of life" and only 11 percent would opt for a "traditional funeral." A shocking 31 percent said they wanted no funeral at all.

I daresay that we as North Americans have become confused. Many of us now believe that having fun, feeling joy and surprise, and being entertained are what having an experience is all about. We have confused honoring with celebration and celebration with partying. And regretfully, we've transferred this idea onto funerals. To borrow a phrase from the musical group R.E.M., we "shiny, happy people" have forgotten that the purpose of a funeral is to mourn—to actively and outwardly embrace the death of someone we love.

The Latin word for celebrate is "celebrare" or "to honor." The colloquial definition is to "have a good time." Yet our true intention when someone loved dies is not to have a good time, but to honor our loved one. This is where the confusion lies. Therefore, when we simply go along with a family's initial request to create a celebration for the person who died, we are not giving them what they truly, deep-down want and need.

What reinforces this desire for celebration is that mourning is painful and not something people readily sign up to do. We are too eager to praise mourners who "stay strong" and "get over it" and "find closure" quickly. Our society has become increasingly mourning-avoidant, and with that we have seen a shift toward celebrations. Yet in their attempt to celebrate, families often miss the ancient and still essential purpose of funerals, which is to create an invitation to mourn openly and honestly.

When people do not feel their feelings, they become unable to be changed by them. Instead of experiencing movement through loss, they become stuck. They experience chronic grief that affects all areas of their lives. Of course, meaningful funerals are not devoid of celebration and laughter. As you know, funny anecdotes about the person who died are often a welcome and necessary part of the experience. Authentic, meaningful funerals invite a full range of emotions, from deep sadness, to joy and laughter. This is where your role as an educator and ritual specialist comes into play. When families request celebrations, you can choose to gently guide them toward a funeral that will serve as a catalyst for their mourning, rather than as a tool to suppress it.

Some Good News

Addressing the growing trend toward cremation, some funeral homes have added cremation tribute centers that allow families to participate in the cremation ritual. Others have begun training staff members to plan and lead funeral ceremonies and have trained or hired celebrants, who add depth to funerals by getting to know the family and the person who died intimately and encouraging people to talk about him or her and share memories through stories, anecdotes, and pictures. Celebrants particularly serve those seeking a non-religious, yet spiritual, ceremony. This interfaces with the reality that many baby boomers and Xgeners are spiritual, but not necessarily religious. Some funeral homes have even recreated their funeral arranging process so that it focuses on the unique life of the person who died—not on the filling out of forms.

Throughout this third edition you will find examples of ways in which caregivers to those who mourn are reinvesting themselves in the funeral ritual. Many of the examples come from funeral directors and clergy, because I often have the privilege to speak with them in my travels across North America, but I hope that everyone reading this book will find them inspiring and useful. You will also find an introduction to the concept of creating not just meaningful funeral ceremonies, but meaningful funeral experiences. The experience economy is indeed upon us, and it offers an inspiring model for funeral service in the 21st century.

"Tis the good reader that makes the book," said Ralph Waldo Emerson. That observation applies especially to this type of resource. This text, written for people willing to constantly strive to improve their skills in creating and leading authentic funeral rituals, will do little good if its messages are exiled to the reader's mental bookshelves. Instead I challenge you to consider Creating Meaningful Funeral Experiences each time you plan a new funeral and to persistently and creatively strive to improve your ability to bring meaning to the funeral experiences of those you "walk with" in grief.

My wish for you is that the information and ideas in this book will inspire you to the benefit of those you help. As you read Creating Meaningful Funeral Experiences, I invite you to share your own ideas about funerals with me. Please drop me a note to express your views about this important area of bereavement ministry.

Cordially,

Alan D. Wolfelt, Ph.D.
Director, Center for Loss and Life Transition

April 2011

Introduction

Understanding the Importance of Meaningful Ceremonies

Contemporary times have resulted in many people becoming unaware of meaningful funeral ceremonies. While funerals have been with us since the beginning of human history, many North Americans are now deciding that funeral rituals don't have a place in their lives. We seem to be minimizing, avoiding, and denying the need for rituals surrounding death. More and more, people are saying, "When I die, you can throw a party, but I don't want a funeral."

Death rituals and ceremonies have been with us since the beginning of humankind. Those who have gone before us in this world—in fact, all of our predecessors—embraced both life and death in ceremony. Rituals were a central part of everyday life, whether it was acknowledging new life, sharing a meal together, celebrating the harvest or burying the dead. New life, loss of life and most every major life transition were met with ceremony.

Yet in recent years, more and more North Americans are questioning the value of planning and participating in ceremonies that honor the "rites of passage" from life to death. There is an unfortunate perception the "educated" and "sophisticated" people are somehow above the need to openly express grief through public ceremony. A continuing trend is to dispose of the dead and quickly return to normal life. The problem: If we don't acknowledge the significance of death, we don't acknowledge the significance of life!

We live in an efficiency-seeking society that values convenience. People send the message to their friends and family to not bother when they die. Many ask for no funeral, requesting that families celebrate their lives, instead. Families welcome this philosophy. It's tidy, and it fits with the idea that if we just keep moving and stay busy, this messy business of grieving can't catch up with us.

People may no longer understand that to heal, they must go through hurt. Yet it is in dosing themselves with hurt and the emotions of sadness, pain, and loss that people find that "sweet spot" of meaning during a ceremony. While people may not readily recognize it, they often feel unfulfilled after a ceremony or party that leaves no space for mourning. Their internal feelings over the death are inconsistent with the external response to it. In other words, they experience an absence of meaning.

When facilitators and funeral arrangers produce a meaningful ceremony, as outlined in this book, they invite mourners into "liminal space"—a spiritual place betwixt and between, where most people are uncomfortable being, but one that leads them toward eventual integration of the loss into their lives.

Meaningful funerals incorporate not only a celebration but invite those attending to mourn, and in doing so, help them begin to accept the grief process that's upon them. While it isn't always immediately apparent to families that they need a meaningful experience, the memories of it afterwards provide a lasting, healing effect.

The goal of a meaningful funeral ceremony is not closure—it is to create divine momentum toward healing and move mourners toward transformation so they can open to the experience of grief.

As a death educator and grief counselor, I have become a proud advocate of the vital importance of meaningful funeral ceremonies. While I trained for twelve years to become a "talk therapist," I always say in my workshops that "when words are inadequate, have a ceremony." I have been privileged to companion people in grief for over thirty-five years now. The longer I am involved in this ministry, the more convinced I am that well-planned, purposeful funerals are a sacred necessity to helping people of all ages, genders, and cultures to integrate death into their lives. A meaningful funeral is essential to the healing of broken hearts. No, the funeral doesn't create "closure" but instead creates divine momentum toward healing by establishing a "meaningful beginning" for mourners. Life is never quite the same after someone loved dies. The meaning of the life lost deserves to be honored in an appropriately remarkable way. Meaningful funerals connect us with our past, with those we love, and with the greater meaning of life. Most importantly, meaningful funerals help us say hello on the pathway to goodbye!

Understanding the Cremation Trend

The Cremation Association of North America reports that in 2008, 35.79 percent of all the people who died in the U.S. were cremated, up from the 1960 figure

Cremation Rates in the United States		Cremation Rates in Canada	
1960	3.56%	1960	3.25%
1970	4.59%	1970	5.89%
1980	9.72%	1980	18.85%
1990	17.13%	1990	32.54%
2000	26.24%	1999	46.2%
2009	36.86% (estimated)	2009	68.4% (estimated)
2015	46.04% (projected)	2015	85+% (projected)
2025	58.85% (projected)	2025	(unavailable)

Source: The Cremation Association of North America www.cremationassociation.org

(A regional caveat: The use of cremation varies greatly by region. In the U.S., for example, states with 2008 rates higher than 65 percent included Nevada, Hawaii, Oregon, and Washington. On the opposite end of the spectrum were Alabama, Mississippi, Georgia, and Kentucky—all with cremation rates less than 15 percent. In Canada, the 2000 rates for New Brunswick were 21.4 percent (projected to be 53.5 percent in 2015), whereas the rates for British Columbia were 75.7 percent in 2000 (projected to be 83 percent in 2015).

of 3.56 percent. The same organization projects the U.S. cremation rate will surpass 46.04 percent by the year 2015, and 58.85 percent by 2025. The Canadian figures (see accompanying graph) mirror and even outpace this trend.

What's troubling about this overall trend toward cremation? Many North Americans who choose cremation also choose not to have an accompanying service, thereby avoiding the funeral ritual altogether. While we do not know what portion of the current 36 percent receives direct cremation with no funeral service, my experience with the funeral service suggests that many of the growing numbers of North Americans requesting cremation do not partake in an accompanying ritual. Again, they carry out what is called "direct cremation."

Yet this may be changing. According to a 15-year study released in 2010 by the Funeral and Memorial Information Council (FAMIC), 94 percent of study participants who said they would choose cremation for a loved one indicated they planned to have "some sort" of funeral or memorial service to commemorate the life of their loved one. Depending on how these self-reported preferences actually unfold, that's good news for families grieving the loss of a loved one. (As an interesting side note, rates for planned cremations were higher than those projected by CANA: 55 percent of the 500 survey respondents said they would likely or definitely choose cremation for a loved one. This signifies that the trend toward cremation may be even stronger than current projections indicate.)

In cultures where cremation is an ancient practice, as in India and Japan, it is accompanied by powerful symbolism of release, purification, and unity. As Thomas Lynch, funeral director and author, recently said, "The problem is not that we cremate our dead, but how ritually denatured, spiritually vacant, religiously timid, and impoverished we have allowed the practice to become. It is not that we do it, but how we do it that must be reconsidered."

Many would attribute the rise in direct cremation to the perceived high costs of today's traditional funeral. On the contrary, the 2010 FAMIC study showed that just 33 percent of the people electing cremation do so because of the financial considerations. Another 12 percent chose cremation for environmental considerations.

This is certainly not to say that cremation as a form of disposition is inherently bad; when used together with ceremony, cremation can be a part of a beautiful funeral experience. In fact, used creatively and flexibly, cremation can actually increase an at-need family's ceremony options. Fortunately, more and more funeral homes are now integrating Cremation Tribute Centers

In 2008, 71 percent of deaths were casketed, according to the Casket & Funeral Supply Association of America, a 5 percent decrease since 2003.

that house a crematory, a Witness Room a small family conference room and a Gathering Room for visitations and receptions.

Incorporating a New Approach to Arranging Meaningful Funeral Experiences

Modern beliefs about funerals are requiring funeral arrangers to adjust their approach. They can no longer rely on the old arrangement model of gathering vital statistics and obituary information, providing service details, taking orders, and selling products. They now must provide a meaningful, lasting experience if they (perhaps you!) are to exist into the future.

According to the Funeralwise.com survey, many people no longer want a traditional funeral and many don't want a funeral at all. Doubt in the value of the funeral is rampant, and if families don't sense an underlying passion for and commitment to the whys of funeral service when they walk through your doors, they will walk out your doors just as—if not more—unimpressed with funerals. Get clear on the why. Ask yourself these questions: Why do you do what you do? Why are meaningful funerals important? What is your role in helping families create a funeral experience? Why did you come to work this morning? Why did you get in this line of work? Your most honest answers to these simple questions reveal a lot about you and why you do what you do. You see, why you do what you do is more important than what you do and how you do it.

This new approach demands that funeral arrangers internalize the belief that their job is first and foremost about helping people manage the deeply-human experience of the death of someone loved. Simon Sinek, a marketing consultant known for creating the Golden Circle concept of business success, professes that if we are to truly succeed and lead, we must act from the inside out, not from the outside in. In other words, as businesspeople and caregivers we must start with our core beliefs, purposes, and intentions. From there, we take actions to support our beliefs, and from those actions we gain tangible results. As Sinek says, "People don't buy what you do. They buy why you do it, and what you do simply serves as the proof of what you believe." So I challenge you to think about the following: What is your funeral home's cause? What is your career cause, your calling? What brings meaning to your work? Your deep-down cause and passion is your why. And if your why is grounded in the essential, healing reasons we as a people have had funerals since the beginning of time, you have the potential to inspire and reengage your community.

Yet in my work with thousands of grieving people, I have found that, in general, people do not understand why funeral ceremonies help us adapt to change and help us heal. That is, until they experience a meaningful funeral service, themselves. Then they begin to understand. The good news is that our society's tendency to diminish the importance of the funeral ritual—a trend that to me seemed to have taken on alarming proportions in the late 20th century—may now be showing early signs of reversing. At least, that is my hope and my prayer.

According to the 2010 FAMIC study, people clearly understand the importance of funerals and rituals: 92 percent of respondents 40 and older who had recently attended a funeral said "the funeral industry provides meaning and value to the arrangement process," an increase from 86 percent in 2004. Of those respondents, 95 percent of surveyed people who recently attended a funeral said that the ceremony helped them pay tribute to the person who died. Moreover, 87 percent said that the service played a key role in helping them "begin the healing process" after the death of someone loved.

The next time a family walks through your door, ask yourself, "Why am I right here, right now? Why is my work important? Why is a meaningful funeral service essential?" Live that inner inspiration in every moment with every family. Wear the authentic why on your sleeve and the families you serve will gladly follow you.

Seeing funeral directors, clergy, celebrants, and ritual spiritualists as facilitators and educators who help families create meaningful ceremonies demands that they act as companions and gentle guides. They join the family in their unique journey. They listen carefully, ask questions, and, once they understand the family and the person who died, make suggestions about how to best honor him or her in a profoundly personal way. The five-part arrangement model presented in this book helps arrangers create personalized, meaningful, and memorable events for the families they serve. In doing so, funeral homes will not only provide a framework for creating authentic funerals but survive and thrive.

Influences on the Deritualization of the Funeral

Some years back, a national telephone study was commissioned*, talking with more than 800 consumers 40 and older. Its objective was to better understand consumers' attitudes and beliefs about funerals and funeral products. Under the assumption that a generation's experience of growing up in the same era collectively shapes their thinking, attitudes and behavior, the study analyzed data from a generational perspective rather than breaking out respondents by gender, income or education.

The study looked at "GI Generation" consumers, born 1901-1924; "Silent Generation" consumers, born 1925-1942; and Boomers, born 1943-1964. Of the three groups, the study found Boomers to be much less satisfied with the funerals they had been a part of. They were also dissatisfied with the arrangement process, wanting more information, more time to make the arrangements and more ideas for personalizing the service. Finally, Boomers didn't value the casket nearly as highly.

Boomers are dissatisfied with the [funeral] arrangement process, wanting more information, more time to make the arrangements, and more ideas for personalizing service.

Coupled with these findings about Boomer predilections is the fact that Boomers don't attend many funerals. According to the 2010 Funeral and Memorial Information Council (FAMIC) study on funeral habits, on average Americans attended 1.4 funerals in funeral homes each year. As reported by the National Center for Health Statistics and the U.S. Bureau of the Census, the U.S. death rate (and hence, the funeral rate) is not expected to increase until 2020, when the progressive aging of baby boomers sets in. People today are not accustomed to making funeral arrangements and haven't attended many services. Naturally, this means they are often not aware of the value of funerals.

Almost gone are the days when people make funeral arrangements before their death, setting aside funds, buying plots, and wanting all aspects of a traditional funeral. Today, most funeral decisions are driven by those left behind—Boomers, X-geners and Y-geners. As David A. Casper, Managing Funeral Director with Casper Funeral Services in Boston recently wrote in his organization's newsletter, "Now more than ever funerals are generation-driven. Each generation's approach to funeral spending [and ritual decisions] will continue to

*The study was sponsered by Batesville Casket Company.

change the funeral service provider's choices." Casper finds that X-geners tend to lean toward funerals with fewer enhancements, and even more so, Y-geners.

Often, for people from current generations traditional funeral rituals are devoid of value and meaning. They perceive them as empty and lacking creativity. I don't blame them. I myself have attended way too many of what I would term generic funerals—cookie cutter ceremonies that leave you feeling like you may as well have been at a stranger's funeral. As more and more people attend these meaningless funerals, society's opinion of the funeral suffers. This in turn causes people to devalue the funeral that will be held for them someday: "When I die, don't go to any trouble." A tendency to minimize one's own funeral is for many a reflection of the sense of purposelessness they have witnessed while attending generic funeral services.

But we as humans weren't born questioning the need for funerals. Products of the times in which they were born, they grew into this mindset. Here are some of the influences that have shaped people's likes and dislikes, wants and needs, concerning funerals.

- **We live in the world's first death-free generation.**
  Many people now live into their 40s and 50s before they experience a close personal loss. Today two-thirds of all deaths in the U.S. each year happen to people 65 or older. One result of this mortality rate shift is that if you are forty or older and have never attended a truly meaningful funeral, you probably don't realize the importance of having one.

  "To forget one's ancestors is to be a brook without a source, a tree without a root."
  – Chinese proverb

  In the early 1900s, on the other hand, most children had been to many funerals by the age of ten. (In 1900 over half of all deaths in the U.S. each year were deaths of children 15 or younger.) Aging, illness and death were an everyday part of family life. While we certainly appreciate the medical advances that have helped lower the mortality rate and prolong lifespans, they are also distancing us from aging, illness, death, grief—and thus the funeral ritual.

- **We live in a mobile, fast-paced culture.**
  Tremendous geographical distances often separate family members and friends today. Fifty years ago, friends only had to walk down the street to be a part of a funeral; now it is not unusual for them to fly in from thousands of miles away. This isn't convenient, and we are a convenience-based culture. If it isn't easy, we often just don't do it.

  The Industrial Revolution brought about mass production and with it an emphasis on speed, efficiency and productivity. Then came the Techno-

Revolution, heightening our ability to work faster, travel faster, communicate faster. We have come not just to want but to expect instant gratification—overnight delivery, cellular telephones, e-mail in a second, microwave popcorn, digital photos, instant credit and home pregnancy tests. Other time-compressed, mind-shifting technologies include instant, worldwide news, video teleconferencing and hamburgers in less than 90 seconds.

These examples of instant gratification change our frame of reference, our expectations, our values. Partly because we're busier and partly because we've come to expect it, we demand faster ways of doing things. And, unfortunately, we often confuse efficiency with effectiveness. When people get too busy, the first thing to go are rituals—from eating together to vacations to attending funerals.

- **We're disconnected from each other.**

For starters, many people have lost a sense of community. Not long ago, people shared their lives with those around them. Generation after generation, families lived in the same town or at least the same state. Neighbors visited on the front porch, gathered for meals and took care of each other's children. People knew each other. People watched out for each other. People cared about each other. Now, like no other time in history, many people feel alone and unconnected to groups.

"When a person is born, we rejoice. When they are married, we celebrate. When they die, we pretend nothing happened."
– Margaret Mead

One study found that 71 percent of Americans didn't know their neighbors. Adults and children alike live among strangers. The number of people who report they never spend time with their neighbors has doubled in only the last twenty years.

What's more, in the beginning of this century, only ten percent of people lived in big cities. Now, over forty percent do. The irony is that when more people lived outside the city there was a greater sense of community.

We have evolved from a country of primary relationships to one of secondary relationships. Primary relationships are ones in which people know each other in a variety of roles—as friends, neighbors, co-workers. Secondary relationships are ones in which people are merely acquaintances. We may sit next to someone at work, but often we don't know much about him—where he lives, if he has a family, what his hobbies are.

As we have connected to the Internet, we have disconnected from each other. Names on the Net aren't always even real names. Our state-of-the-art technology has created a new kind of person, one who is plugged into machines instead of fellow human beings. Some of us talk more to voicemail then we do to our own family members.

- **We value self-reliance.**

  Have you noticed that the biggest section in bookstores these days is the self-help section? We live in an era of rugged individualism and independence. We reward people for "doing it on their own." How many of us grew up learning the North American motto, "If you want it done right, do it yourself"? Yet, when someone in your life dies, you must be interdependent and connected to the world around you if you are to heal. In short, rugged individualism and funerals don't mix well.

- **We eschew spiritualism.**

  As our society becomes more educated, we seem to be adopting a more academic orientation to life and death. As I travel throughout North America, I observe that some of the largest pocket areas of direct cremation with no ceremony are in highly populated, academic communities. In a 1962 study, sociologist Robert Fulton confirmed that people who doubt the usefulness of funerals are more likely to be highly educated, professionally employed and financially well off. Observational research of today is consistent with Fulton's 50-year-old findings.

  Of course, many among this highly educated population would argue they have found a substitute for the old-fashioned, "morbid" funeral: the memorial service or "celebration of life." It seems that the more educated one becomes, the more "at risk" one becomes for not participating in death rituals. The potential problem with memorial services is twofold: 1) they are often delayed until a more convenient time weeks or months after the death; and 2) the body is often not present. These factors tend to encourage mourners to skirt the healing pain that funerals—because of their timeliness, their focus on embracing a variety of feelings, including pain (not just joy), and their use of the body as reality check—set in motion. (See the section on symbolism, p. 15.) How many times have you heard someone leave a memorial service or celebration saying, "Wasn't that great? No one even cried!" While some memorials or celebrations of life are certainly meaningful and authentic, I am suggesting that sometimes they do healthy mourning a disservice.

- **We don't understand the role of pain and suffering.**

  Another major influence on the deritualization of death in our culture is our avoidance of pain. We misunderstand the role of suffering. People who openly express their feelings of grief are often told to "carry on", "keep your chin up" or "just keep busy." Worse yet, some bereaved people are greeted with theologized clichés like "God wouldn't give you any more than you can bear," and "Look at it this way . . . now you have an angel in heaven." This misuse of doctrine is used by some for the purpose of suppressing "incorrect" thoughts and feelings.

  Shame-based messages like the above examples result in some bereaved people thinking that mourning (i.e. sharing your grief outside yourself) is bad.

If you are perceived as "doing well" with your grief, on the other hand, you are considered "strong" and "under control." Of course, it is easier to stay "rational" if you don't participate in a ceremony that is intended to, among other things, encourage you to embrace feelings and acknowledge a painful reality.

- **We have lost the symbolism of death.**

Deritualization also appears to be influenced by a loss of death's symbols. Ariès, in his book *The Hour of Our Death*, identifies the symbols representing death in art and in literature, as well as in funeral and burial customs. He maintains, and I agree, that symbols of death are no longer prominent in contemporary North American culture, and that gone with them is a link that in previous generations provided meaning and a sense of continuity for the living.

In generations past, for example, the bereaved used to wear mourning clothes or armbands, often black, that symbolized their sorrow. In some subcultures, mourners also hung wreaths on the door to let others know that someone loved had died. Today we can't even tell who the bereaved are. For some, memorial flowers, both at the funeral and at the cemetery, are becoming another ousted symbol. Today we opt for the more practical but less spiritual monetary donation: "In lieu of flowers, please send contributions to…"

Perhaps the ultimate symbol of death that we are tending more and more to forsake is the dead person's body.

Perhaps the ultimate symbol of death that we are tending more and more to forsake is the dead person's body. When viewed at the visitation or during the funeral service itself, the body encourages mourners to confront the reality and the finality of the death. Of course, opponents of viewing often describe it as unseemly, expensive, undignified and unnecessary. Yet, seeing and spending time with the body allows for last goodbyes and visual confirmation that someone loved is indeed dead. I often say that it is a part of the hello on the pathway to goodbye. In generations past, the body often served as the very centerpiece of mourning; the bereaved came to the dead person's home to view the body, pay their last respects and support the primary mourners. In fact, the body was often displayed for days before burial. Today, with our increasing reliance on closed caskets and direct cremation with no services, we are forgetting the importance of this tradition.

As Ariès writes, "The function or value (in death's role in our society) consists precisely in banishing from the sight of the public not only death but with it, its icon. Relegated to the secret, private space of the home or the anonymity of the hospital, death no longer makes any sign." As we eliminate the symbols of death, we also appear to be eliminating the rituals, historically rich in symbolism, that remind us of the death of others as well as our own mortality.

Recently, in a very wise observation Thomas G. Long noted, "For the first time in history, the actual presence of the dead at their own funerals has become optional, even undesirable, lest the body break the illusion of a cloudless celebration. [There is a fear that having the body present will] spoil the meditative mood and reveal the truths about grief, life and death that our thinned-out ceremonies can't bear."

- **We deny our own mortality.**
  One woman once said to me, "I don't do death." She is not alone. Many people in North America today deny their own mortality and thus the need for rituals surrounding death. In his book *The Funeral: Vestige or Value*, author Paul Irion calls this "assumed invulnerability." He reflects that, "Man knows that he is only assuming invulnerability, that he is ultimately vulnerable, and yet to admit this fact totally is to be defenseless." In other words, denying our own mortality is better than the alternative.

  "Man knows that he is only assuming invulnerability, that he is ultimately vulnerable, and yet to admit this fact totally is to be defenseless."
  – Paul Irion

  Sigmund Freud also wrote of this theme in his *Collected Papers* when he concluded, "At bottom no one believes in his own death, or to put the same thing in another way, in the unconscious every one of us is convinced of his own immortality."

- **We're devaluing life.**
  Sad to say, but many children and adults have become desensitized to the meaning and value of life as well as death. I recently read about a new fad on school playgrounds. Children are bringing laser pens to school and using them for pretend "lasergunfights" at recess. The tragic and all-too-real school shootings in recent years only compound the irony of this violent play.

  Television has presented a distorted image of the significance of a human life. Simply by turning on the TV, we are exposed to a multitude of examples of violent death each day. All too often, themes of violence take center stage in our books, movies and music, too. Internalizing these powerful images can result in a cynical view of life in general, let alone the need to have ceremonies when someone loved dies.

  Many of today's kids are not being taught to value life. How are they ever to learn to value and respect death?

- **We're forgetting our values.**
  Many North Americans appear to be facing an enemy from within—a crisis of meaning and values.

The media teaches us to value consumerism, as if we can somehow buy our happiness. Many children would rather watch TV than go for a walk in the woods. Some children and adults have been coerced by the media into believing they should meet every want, buy every product, and do it now. As the Nike commercial says, "Just Do It!"

Many families have become disconnected from each other and the natural world. Did you know that one in three children live apart from their biological father in the U.S., according to 2009 Census Bureau data? That's a substantial increase from 1960, when only one-in-ten children lived in homes without fathers. Values that were once taught by family, church and community are now, more often that not, taught through advertisements and mindless TV sitcoms.

Our culture of immediate gratification, self-absorption, and deceit has confused us about what is right and wrong and good and bad. Many people don't have road maps for what family life should be like, let alone what a meaningful funeral should be like.

These are some of the most prominent reasons for the current North American trend toward the deritualization of death. Give thought to what other influences may be impacting the deritualization of our culture and note them here.

____

____

____

____

____

____

____

____

In her book *Brit-Think, America-Think*, author Jane Walmsley summed up well the current North American mindset about death: "The single most important thing to know about Americans . . . is that they think death is optional." Unfortunately, today we do believe that mourning, if it is to be done at all, should be done quickly and privately—three days off work then back to the normal routine. No time for planning ceremonies. No need to befriend the pain. No time to say hello on the pathway to goodbye. Should these messages continue to be internalized, we may well see the continued deritualization of death in our culture. My hope is that we can all join forces to reverse this trend as we advocate for authentic, meaningful funeral experiences.

"Primitive man faced his grief directly and worked out a system of personal and social rituals and symbols that made it possible for him to deal with it directly. Modern man does not seem to know how to proceed in the expression of this fundamental emotion. He has not generally accepted social patterns for dealing with death. His rituals are partial and unsatisfying. His funerals are apt to be meaningless and empty. Either he is so afraid of normal emotion that his funerals are sterile, or they are so steeped in superficialities that they remain meaningless, and the more normal emotions remain unengaged."
– Reverend Edgar Jackson

Funeral Misconceptions

- Funerals are too expensive. The social, psychological and emotional benefits of authentic funerals far outweigh their financial costs. Besides, a funeral needn't be lavishly expensive to be meaningful.
- Funerals make us too sad. When someone loved dies, we need to be sad. Funerals provide us with a safe place in which to embrace our pain.
- Funerals are barbaric. On the contrary, meaningful funeral ceremonies are civilized, socially binding rituals. Some people think that viewing the body is barbaric. Cultural differences aside, viewing has many benefits for survivors. (See p. 15.)
- Funerals are inconvenient. Taking a few hours out of your week to demonstrate your love for the person who died and your support for survivors is not an inconvenience but a privilege.
- Funerals and cremation are mutually exclusive. A funeral (with or without the body present) may be held prior to cremation. Embalmed bodies are often cremated.
- Funerals require the body to be embalmed. Not necessarily. Depending on local regulations, funerals held shortly after the death may require no special means of preservation.
- Funerals are only for religious people. Not true. Non-religious ceremonies (which, by the way, need not be held in a church or officiated by a clergy person) can still meet the survivors' mourning needs as discussed in Part 2 of this resource.
- Funerals are rote and meaningless. They needn't be. With forethought and planning, funerals can and should be personalized rituals reflecting the uniqueness of the bereaved family.
- Funerals should reflect what the dead person wanted. Not really . . . While pre-planning your funeral may help you reconcile yourself to your own mortality, funerals are primarily for the benefit of the living.
- Funerals are only for grown-ups. Anyone old enough to love is old enough to mourn. Children, too, have the right and the privilege to attend funerals. (See more on children and funerals, p. 73.)

Exploring the Purposes of Meaningful Funeral Ceremonies

Rituals are symbolic experiences that help us, together with our families and friends, express our deepest thoughts and feelings about life's most important events. Baptism celebrates the birth of a child and that child's acceptance into the church family. Birthday parties honor the passing of another year in the life of someone we love. Weddings publicly affirm the private love shared by two people.

Spend a moment thinking about other rituals, religious or secular, past or present, that humankind has created to express that which it could not express otherwise. Consider, too, the rituals that have lent meaning to your life. Jot down a few notes here.

What do such rituals have in common? First, they are typically public events. Families, friends, church members, villages, even nations—any group with strong emotional or philosophical ties—may create and enact a ritual, providing a support system for common beliefs and values. Rituals unite us.

Second, most rituals follow an established, cultural-specific procedure. American high school graduations, for example, begin with a procession of students in cap and gown, include one or more speeches and culminate when the graduates march across a platform to accept their diplomas. As with all rituals, the details will change somewhat from graduation to graduation, but the general pattern always remains recognizable. The predictability of ritual helps participants feel at ease. It also lends a sense of continuity, of the distillation of generations past, to those events we find most meaningful.

Finally, and perhaps most important, rituals are symbolic. Wedding rings, christening gowns, mortarboards and gold watches all symbolize important life transitions and commitments. Not just the objects but also the very acts of ritual are symbolic, as well. We blow out candles at birthday parties, for example, to symbolize the completion of another year. At a graduation ceremony's end, the graduates toss their caps into the air to symbolize their newfound freedom. What words could we possibly utter that would capture so well our feelings at these moments? Ritualistic behavior is an effort to act out things that are difficult, if not impossible, to put into words. The symbol of ritual provides us a means to express our beliefs and feelings when language alone will not do those beliefs and feelings justice.

The funeral ritual, too, is a public, traditional and symbolic means of expressing our beliefs, thoughts and feelings about the death of someone loved. Rich in history and rife with symbolism, the funeral ceremony helps us acknowledge the reality of the death, gives testimony to the life of the deceased, encourages the expression of grief in a way consistent with the culture's values, provides support to mourners, allows for the embracing of faith and beliefs about life and death, and offers continuity and hope for the living.

Now, let's look more specifically at the many purposes of the funeral. I have discovered that a helpful way to teach about the functions of authentic funeral ceremonies is to frame them up in the context of the "reconciliation needs of

---

Reconciliation versus Resolution

In many grief models, the final dimension of bereavement is referred to as resolution. Other paradigms use the terms recovery, re-establishment or reorganization. The problem with this dimension as defined in these ways is that people do not "get over" grief.

Reconciliation is a term I find more appropriate for what occurs as the bereaved person works to integrate the new reality of moving forward in life without the physical presence of the person who has died. With reconciliation comes a renewed sense of energy and confidence, an ability to fully acknowledge the reality of the death, and a capacity to become reinvolved in the activities of living.

As the experience of reconciliation unfolds, the mourner recognizes that life will be different without the presence of the person who died. The sharp, ever-present pain of grief gives rise to a renewed sense of meaning and purpose. The feeling of loss does not completely disappear, yet softens, and the intense pangs of grief become less frequent. Hope for a continued life emerges as the griever is able to make commitments to the future, realizing that the dead person will never be forgotten, yet knowing that one's own life can and will move forward.

---

mourning"—my twist on what other author's have called the "tasks of mourning." The reconciliation needs of mourning are the six needs that I believe to be the most central to healing in grief. In other words, bereaved people who have these needs met, through their own grief work and through the love and compassion of those around them, are most often able to reconcile their grief and go on to find continued meaning in life and living.

As you read this section, please keep in mind that a meaningful ceremony is but one of many elements that influence a bereaved person's ability to have his or her grief needs met. Obviously, healing in grief is not an event but a process that will unfold for weeks, months and even years after the funeral itself. The funeral is a ritual of ending, but it only marks the beginning of the healing process. Even so, a meaningful funeral can certainly begin to meet all six reconciliation needs, setting the tone for the grief journey to come.

Here I would also like to introduce the concept of "dosing" grief. The bereaved cannot deal with their grief all at once; if they tried to, they would die. Instead, they must "dose" their grief by allowing in the pain and other strong emotions a bit at a time. The meaningful funeral allows mourners to get one of their first doses of grief and life as it now will be in the context of a social support system. To take the medicinal analogy of dosing one step further, the funeral provides us with a supportive atmosphere in which to take the initial pain of our grief, much as our parents provided us with soothing words and loving caresses when as children we had to take our medicine.

How the authentic funeral helps meet the six reconciliation needs of mourning

Mourning Need #1. Acknowledge the reality of the death.

When someone loved dies, we must openly acknowledge the reality and the finality of the death if we are to move forward with our grief. Typically, we embrace this reality in two phases. First we acknowledge the death with our minds; we are told that someone we love has died and, intellectually at least, we understand the fact of the death. Over the course of the following days and weeks, and with the gentle understanding of those around us, we begin to acknowledge the reality of the death in our hearts.

The Difference Between *Grief* and *Mourning*

Let's remind ourselves of the important distinction between the terms grief and mourning. Grief is the internal thoughts and feeling of loss and pain, whereas mourning is the outward, shared expression of that grief—or grief gone public. All bereaved families grieve when someone they love dies. But if they are to heal, they must have a safe, accepting atmosphere in which they can mourn. A meaningful funeral can provide them with such an atmosphere for expression of their early grief.

Meaningful funeral ceremonies can serve as wonderful points of departure for "head understanding" of the death. Intellectually, funerals teach us that someone we loved is now dead, even though up until the funeral we may have denied this fact. When we contact the funeral home, set a time for the service, plan the ceremony, view the body, perhaps even choose clothing and jewelry for the body, we cannot avoid acknowledging that the person has died. When we see the casket being lowered into the ground, we are witness to death's finality.

"Rituals build community, creating a meeting-ground where people can share deep feelings, positive and negative, a place where they can sing or scream, howl ecstatically or furiously, play, or keep a solemn silence."
– Starhawk

Though I have already touched on this point in this book's first section (see p. 15), here I would like to reemphasize the importance of open casket visitations and funeral services to the need to acknowledge the reality of the death. For mourners, to be invited to see the body is to be invited to say goodbye and to touch one last time that person they loved so much. It is also to be invited to confront our disbelief that someone we cared deeply about is gone and cannot return. Far from being morbid or carnivalesque, open casket services help us acknowledge the reality of the death and transition from life as it was then to life as it is now. As author Thomas Lynch astutely noted, "Can you have a funeral without a dead guy there? No, you can't. That's the essential manifest. You might have a very nice event, but it is not a funeral."

Of course, we must respect cultural and religious differences concerning the treatment of and focus on the body. Judaism, for example, prohibits embalming or any cosmetic "restoration." Viewing of the body is seen as a violation of the rights of the dead. However, the general North American trend away from viewing the body is a trend to be concerned about.

Mourning Need #2. Move toward the pain of the loss.
As our acknowledgment of the death progresses from what I call "head understanding" to "heart understanding," we begin to embrace the pain of the loss—another need the bereaved must have met if they are to heal. Healthy grief means expressing our painful thoughts and feelings, and meaningful funeral ceremonies allow us to do just that.

People tend to cry, even sob and wail, at funerals because funerals force us to concentrate on the fact of the death and our feelings, often excruciatingly painful, about that

"At the time when one should be joyous—be joyous. And when it is time to mourn—mourn."
– Midrash: Genesis Rabai 27:7

"Your pain is the breaking of the shell that encloses your understanding."
– Kahlil Gibran

Expressing Pain Through Keening

Keening is a process of lamenting for the dead. It is usually expressed in a very loud, wailing voice or sometimes in a wordless crying out. Some cultures encourage and legitimize keening, while others don't understand it and sometimes perceive it as "pathological." Ireland, Crete, China and Mexico are among those countries where you are more likely to see the bereaved keening.

Some of us in North America have keened but may have not known the term for what we were doing. I myself

find that when I experience overwhelming grief, there is almost an instinctive, uncalculated crying out. I see this vocalization as a form of protesting a reality I would rather not be confronting. Discharging energy in this way helps me survive. In fact, learning from other cultures about the value of keening may help us uptight North Americans give ourselves permission to surrender to this "wordless cry."

death. For at least an hour or two—longer for mourners who plan the ceremony or attend the visitation—those attending the funeral are not able to intellectualize or distance themselves from the pain of their grief. To their credit, funerals also provide us with an accepted venue for our painful feelings. They are perhaps the only time and place, in fact, during which we as a society condone such openly outward expression of our sadness.

"We must listen to the music of the past to sing in the present and dance into the future."
– The Journey Through Grief

"Little by little, step by step,
I learned that I didn't need
To hang on to the death
To remember the life.
What a joyous discovery."
– Katie Brown McGowin

Mourning Need #3. Remember the person who died.

To heal in grief, we must shift our relationship with the person who died from one of physical presence to one of memory. The authentic funeral encourages us to begin this shift, for it provides a natural time and place for us to think about the moments we shared—good and bad—with the person who died. Like no other time before or after the death, the funeral invites us to focus on our past relationship with that one, single person and to share those memories with others.

At funerals, the eulogy or period of remembrance attempts to highlight the major events in the life of the person who died and the characteristics that he or she most prominently displayed. This is helpful to mourners, for it tends to prompt more intimate, individualized memories. Later, after the ceremony itself, many mourners will informally share memories of the person who died. This, too, is meaningful. Throughout our grief journeys, the more we are able "tell the story"—of the death itself, of our memories of the person who died—the more likely we will be to reconcile our grief. Moreover, the sharing of memories at the funeral affirms the worth we have placed on the person who died, legitimizing our pain. Often, too, the memories others choose to share with us at the funeral are memories that we have not heard before. This teaches us about the dead person's life apart from ours and allows us glimpses into that life that we may cherish forever.

Mourning Need #4. Develop a new self-identity.
Another primary reconciliation need of mourning is the development of a new self-identity. We are all social beings whose lives are given meaning in relation to the lives of those around us. I am not just Alan Wolfelt, but a son, a brother, a husband, a father, a friend. When someone close to me dies, my self-identity as defined in those ways changes.

Van Gennep, in his book *The Rites of Passage*, emphasized that funerals help mourners with their changed statuses. He pointed out that rites of birth, marriage and death mark separation from an old status, transition into a new status and incorporation into that new status. To use his term, funerals are a "rite of passage." In *The Ritual Process*, Turner reminded us that change in an individual's life is a potential threat to the whole social group, which knows how to treat someone in a clearly defined state but not someone who hovers between states.

The funeral helps us begin this difficult process of developing a new self-identity because it provides a social venue for public acknowledgment of our new roles. If you are a parent of a child and that child dies, the funeral marks the beginning of your life as a former parent (in the physical sense; you will always have that relationship through memory). Others attending the funeral are in effect saying, "We acknowledge your changed identity and we want you to know we still care about you." On the other hand, in situations where there is no funeral, the social group does not know how to relate to the person whose identity has changed and often that person is socially abandoned. In addition,

---

Do Funerals Over-idealize the Person Who Died?

Sometimes people feel uncomfortable when they attend the funeral of someone for whom they had mixed feelings: "Good father, loving husband, faithful friend—that's not the Joe I knew!" I have found that this funereal tendency to idealize the person who died helps mourners—primary mourners, especially—better cope with their initial feelings of loss and pain. So Joe wasn't always the greatest guy, but if you were his wife of 35 years, you don't need a rundown of his faults at the funeral. Instead, you need to feel that others loved Joe, too, and that they value your love for him.

Yes, funerals sometimes over-idealize the person who died. That's OK. Later on mourners can more privately contend with their ambivalent feelings.

---

having supportive friends and family around us at the time of the funeral helps us realize we literally still exist. This self-identity issue is illustrated by a comment the bereaved often make: "When he died, I felt like a part of me died, too."

Mourning Need #5. Search for meaning.

When someone loved dies, we naturally question the meaning of life and death. Why did this person die? Why now? Why this way? Why does it have to hurt so much? What happens after death? To heal in grief, we must explore these types of questions if we are to become reconciled to our grief. In fact, we must first ask these "why" questions to decide *why* we should go on living before we can ask ourselves *how* we will go on living. This does not mean we must find definitive answers, only that we need the opportunity to think (and feel) things through.

"No one can claim to be wise about life whose wisdom does not include a relationship to death."
– Rabbi Jack Riemer

"The act of living is different all through. Her absence is like the sky, spread all over everything."
– C.S. Lewis

The funeral provides us with such an opportunity. For those who adhere to a specific religious faith, the meaningful funeral will reinforce that faith and provide comfort. Alternatively, it may prompt us to question our faith, which too can be an enriching process. Whether you agree or disagree with the belief system upheld by a particular funeral service may not matter; what may matter more is that you have held up your heart to that belief system and struggled with the gap.

On a more fundamental level, the funeral reinforces one central fact of our existence: We will die. Like living, dying is a natural and unavoidable process. (We North Americans tend not to acknowledge this.) Thus the funeral helps us search for meaning in the life and death of the person who died as well as in our own lives and impending deaths. Each funeral we attend serves as a sort of dress rehearsal for our own.

Funerals are a way in which we as individuals and as a community convey our beliefs and values about life and death. The very fact of a funeral demonstrates that death is important to us. For the living to go on living as fully and as healthily as possible, this is as it should be.

"The confrontation of death gives the most positive reality to life itself. It makes the individual's existence real, absolute and concrete. And my awareness of this gives my existence and what I do each hour an absolute quality."
– Rollo May

Advocating for Funerals in Your Community: Public Speaking to Community Groups

As a funeral facilitator, part of your role is to advocate in your community for meaningful funeral experiences. After all, now more than ever, the public needs to be educated about the purposes of funerals and how to make them meaningful. One of the most important ways you can contribute to this most important cause is public speaking to community groups.

Many community groups are always looking for people to provide talks for meetings. Put together a letter or brochure describing your availability to talk to groups about why funerals have been with us since the beginning of time. Provide them with several sample titles of talks you can give. For example: "Why I'm Proud To Be A Funeral Officiant," "Creating Meaningful Funeral Ceremonies," "Understanding the Needs of Mourners."

Encourage them to call you to schedule a talk. Get this letter/brochure out to as many potential sources in your service area as possible. You may be surprised by the calls you will get requesting your services. Better yet, when you go out and do a great job, word of mouth spreads and more people will call.

Planning an Exciting Talk

The basics of providing stimulating talks have been with us since Aristotle wrote his book *Rhetoric* twenty-four hundred years ago:

1. Develop a Central Theme

Before you speak, have in mind a clear theme. If you lose focus, you will lose your audience. Make your language simple and understandable. Speak from your heart, not just your head. Put the ideas you will convey down on paper, and practice, practice, practice!

2. Determine Who Your Audience Is

You are trying to achieve two things with every audience you have the honor of speaking to—understanding and acceptance. You want your ideas to be heard and understood by everyone you speak to. And you want your ideas to be accepted. Otherwise, why would you go to the work to talk to them? To achieve understanding and acceptance, it is vital to know your audience.

How do you learn about your audience? Here is a list of questions to consider using in your preparation:

* What is the purpose of this group? Why do they meet together?
* How many people will be there? (The smaller the group, the less formal your talk will be.)
* What educational and cultural backgrounds are they? (Be sensitive to these issues.)

* What experience do they have with your topic? (If they are mid-40s and younger, they may not have been to very many funerals.)
* What do they know about you? (How should you be introduced to the group?)

3. Creating a Beginning, Middle, and End

A good talk generally has three essential parts—beginning, middle, and end.

The beginning must capture the attention of your audience and introduce your central theme. It must be inspiring enough for the audience to want to listen to the rest. For example, let's say you are going to talk on "Creating Meaningful Funeral Ceremonies." You might open with the following:

"Cultural anthropologist, Margaret Mead was very prophetic when years ago she stated, "When people are born, we rejoice, when they marry, we celebrate; yet, when they die, we pretend nothing happened."

Yes, when someone dies in North America we sometime act as if nothing has happened. One of the ways people do that is by questioning if they should participate in a meaningful funeral ceremony. I'm honored to come before you today to explore why meaningful funeral ceremonies are important to all of us."

This kind of beginning makes people want to "lean in" and listen to more of what you have to say.

The middle of your talk presents your ideas in greater depth. It provides information to support your central idea. It must be attractive enough for your audience to want to listen to the rest.

The mid-section of the above presentation might cover the six central needs of funerals:

1. Acknowledge the reality of the death;
2. Embrace the pain of the loss;
3. Remember the person who died;
4. Develop a new self-identity;
5. Search for meaning; and
6. Receive ongoing support from others.

This kind of mid-section both informs and inspires the audience to think about their own needs when someone they love dies.

An effective ending sums up the central theme and inspires the audience to want to learn more. It provides a powerful close that will really stick in the heads and hearts of your listeners. For example, the ending for the presentation on "Creating Meaningful Funeral Ceremonies" might be something like the following:

(Continued on following page.)

"When someone we love dies, we mourn. When we mourn we need the support and love of those who are close to us. The creation of a meaningful funeral is one important way we can let people know we both need and appreciate their support and love at this difficult time.

Thank you for allowing me to talk about how proud I am to be among those who help people who are "bereaved." I remind you that to be bereaved means "to be torn apart" and "to have special needs." When we are torn apart, one special need we have is the creation of a meaningful funeral." Remember—these three basics are central to a successful talk to members of your community. Some of you are already practicing the principles I've outlined here. If so, congratulations! If not, get going—we must all work together to create value in what we have to offer bereaved families.

Mourning Need #6. Receive ongoing support from others.
As previously noted, funerals are a public means of expressing our beliefs and feelings about the death of someone loved. In fact, funerals are the public venue for offering support to others and being supported in grief, both at the time of the funeral and into the future. Funerals make a social statement that says, "Come support me." Whether they realize it or not, those who choose not to have a funeral are saying, "Don't come support me."

People often attend funerals not for their own benefit (although they sometimes should examine this rationalization) but for the benefit of the primary mourners. An office worker's daughter is killed in a car accident, and although they didn't know the girl, the office worker's colleagues attend the funeral to demonstrate their support. The mother feels grateful and after her (skimpy) bereavement leave, returns to work hoping her grief will be acknowledged. This public affirmation value of funerals cannot be overemphasized.

Funerals let us physically demonstrate our support, too. Sadly, ours is not a demonstrative society, but at funerals we are "allowed" to embrace, to touch, to comfort. Again, words are inadequate so we nonverbally demonstrate our support. This physical show of support is one of the most important healing aspects of meaningful funeral ceremonies.

Another one is the helping relationships that are established at funerals. Friends often seek out ways in which they can help the primary mourners: May I bring the flowers back to the house? Would you like someone to watch little Susie for a few afternoons this week? I'd like to make

"Do not separate yourself from the community."
– Hillel

"It's not that I mind death so much, it's just that I don't want to be there when it happens."
– Woody Allen

a few meals for your family. When might be a good time to bring them over? Friends helping friends and strengthened relationships among the living are invaluable funeral offshoots.

Finally, and most simply, funerals serve as the central gathering place for mourners. When we care about someone who died or his family members, we attend the funeral if at all possible. Our physical presence is our most important show of support for the living. By attending the funeral we let everyone else there know that they are not alone in their grief.

Earlier I asked you to spend a few minutes brainstorming about both society's rituals past and present and the rituals you have found most important in your life. Now, while you're still thinking about the many beneficial purposes of the funeral, take a moment to jot down any additional purposes you can think of:

Summary—Purposes of the Meaningful Funeral

For quick review, I've gleaned the major purposes of the funeral discussed at length in this part of this book and listed them here.

Meaningful funerals . . .

. . . confirm that someone we loved has died.
. . . help us understand that death is final.
. . . allow us to say hello on the pathway to goodbye.
. . . serve as a private and public transition between our lives before the death to our lives after the death.
. . . encourage us to embrace and express our pain.
. . . help us remember the person who died and encourage us to share those memories with others.
. . . offer a time and place for us to talk about the life and death of the deceased.
. . . affirm the worth of our relationship with the person who died.
. . . provide a social support system for us and other mourners.
. . . help integrate mourners back into the community.
. . . allow us to search for meaning in life and death.
. . . reinforce the fact of death in all our lives.
. . . establish ongoing helping relationships among mourners.

Additional Resource—The Purpose of Funerals Poster

I have created a poster for your workplace to help teach about the importance and value of meaningful funerals. The poster will serve to remind you and others of this central theme when planning funerals and ceremonies.

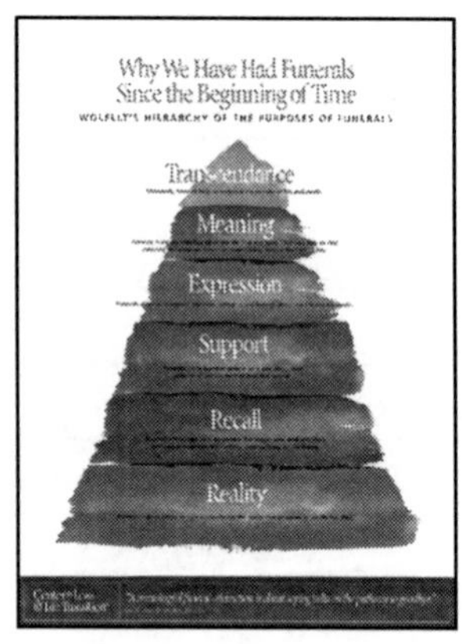

To order copies, contact the Center for Loss and Life Transition at 970-226-6050 or visit my website at www.centerforloss.com.

"Blessed are they that mourn, for they shall be comforted."
– Matthew 5:4

It's the *Experience* that Counts PART 3

I want you to close your eyes and think about the most meaningful days of your life.

Mull these thoughts over for a moment then settle on one certain experience for purposes of this exercise. Perhaps it is your wedding day or the birth of your child. Maybe it is a holiday memory, a special vacation time or a certain afternoon in the company of someone significant to you. Perhaps it is a day spent at the bedside of a loved one who was dying.

The gift of memory is that such experiences live on in us forever.

Do you have a particular experience in mind? Good. Now slowly walk through this memory. What made it so special? Who were you with? Why were you there? What were the surroundings like? What touch sensations do you recall? What sounds can you remember? What smells laced the air? Are there certain tastes you associate with this experience? I'll bet that if you concentrate hard enough and linger long enough in this room of your mind, you'll recall a symphony of sights, sounds, smells, and tastes. You'll remember the thoughts and feelings you had. You may also consider, with the benefit of hindsight, how this experience changed your life.

The gift of memory is that such experiences live on in us forever. Whether joyful or sad, playful or emotionally weighty, memorable experiences form the very fabric of our lives, the warp and weft of who we are.

Sometimes the most memorable experiences of our lives occur spontaneously. Say you are eight years old and in mid-air, jumping off your backyard swing as you have done hundreds of times before. But this time you land akimbo and unbearable pain shoots up your leg. Your discerning mother takes you, sobbing, to the emergency room, where an x-ray reveals you have indeed broken your femur. Suddenly and without warning an everyday experience has become a memorable one.

But perhaps more often, memorable experiences are the product of out-of-the-ordinary, scripted events. Weddings, birthdays, holidays, and vacations often form the backdrop for our most significant memories. As we discussed in Part 2 of this resource, such events are ritualized. They have certain predictable and recognizable patterns and elements that guide us in carrying them out. American birthday parties, for example, require invitations, games and socializing, wrapped presents and a cake alight with candles, which are heartily blown out after a rousing chorus of "Happy Birthday to You."

Which brings me closer to my point. The funeral for someone you love is an out-of-the-ordinary, planned event. It is also a ritualized event, with certain predictable and recognizable patterns and elements. And since the death of someone loved is truly a life-changing experience, the funeral is, by default, a memorable experience.

Think about a funeral that touched you. Why did it touch you? Why was it more memorable than others? Who had died and why? Who was in attendance? What were the surroundings like? What touch sensations do you recall? What sounds can you remember? What smells laced the air? What were your thoughts and feelings at the time?

Here's the heart of the matter. If you agree that memorable experiences shape our lives and that the funeral can be one of life's most memorable experiences, then caregivers who help plan and carry out funerals play an incredibly important role in the community. You have the power to shape people's lives, to orchestrate an exceptional, memorable experience that will help mourners heal and grow.

The Experience Economy (with thanks to Gilmore and Pine)

I've long been a proponent of meaningful funeral ceremonies. I've spoken on this topic to hundreds of funeral directors, clergy and other bereavement caregivers across North America countless times in the last thirty years. But until the 1999 National Funeral Directors Association Convention in Kansas City, when I sat in the audience and listened to keynote speaker and author James Gilmore say, "The Service Economy is peaking. A new, emerging economy is coming to the fore, one based on a distinct kind of economic output (experiences). Goods and services are no longer enough," I hadn't made the connection that what I was championing on behalf of bereaved families was the creation of meaningful funeral experiences.

You have the power to shape people's lives, to orchestrate an exceptional, memorable experience that will help mourners heal and grow.

Of course.

In his speech Gilmore explained how our economy has evolved from being commodities-based to goods-based to service-based, and now, to experience-based. This evolution of economic offerings can itself be instantiated in something as commonplace as the birthday cake.

Gilmore noted that in the agrarian economy, mothers made birthday cakes from scratch, mixing farm commodities (flour, sugar, butter, eggs) that together cost mere pennies. As the goods-based industrial economy advanced, moms paid a dollar or two to Betty Crocker for pre-mixed ingredients. Later, when the service economy took hold, busy parents ordered cakes from the bakery or grocery store, which, at $10 or $15, cost ten times more than the packaged ingredients. Now, in today's time-starved economy, parents neither make the birthday cake nor throw the party. Instead, they spend $100 or more to "outsource" the entire event to Chuck E. Cheese's, the Discovery Zone or some other business that stages memorable events for kids—and often throws in the cake for free.

Experiences, says Gilmore, are a fourth level of value (above commodities, goods and services) and thus can command a much higher price than mere goods or even excellent service. Boomers want and are willing to pay for memorable experiences. They may buy the less expensive toothpaste or contract with the cheapest lawn care service in town, but they are more than willing to pony up for lattés at Starbucks, vacations at Club Med, and the "Total Ownership Experience" of Lexus. Unyoked of the abbreviated lifespans and hardships of generations past, and beneficiaries of the strongest economy in the history of the world, they're more affluent, more educated and more able to turn their attention to "the things that really matter."

And it turns out that the things that really matter—the things that give life meaning—aren't things at all but experiences.

Baby Boomers have unique wants and complaints about funeral service. They typically want more information and more ideas for personalization. They increasingly want cremation. They often don't care about the casket. Some days it feels like they're picking on just funeral service, but they're not. They're voicing similar wants and complaints about restaurants, clothing, education, home design, etc. etc. etc.. Across the board, Boomers want engaging experiences.

So I returned home from the NFDA Convention buzzing with new ideas and connections. And I read Gilmore's book, *The Experience Economy: Work is Theatre & Every Business a Stage* (Harvard Business School Press, 1999), which he coauthored with his business partner, B. Joseph Pine II. I found that the concept of creating meaningful funeral experiences could be further explored in the context of the Experience Economy.

Before we go much further, however, I should point out to you that experiences are not synonymous with entertainment. Don't dismiss the experience concept because it conjures up images of clergy tap-dancing in tails alongside the casket. While the visionary Walt Disney and others who followed in his footsteps certainly foresaw and capitalized on the value of entertaining experiences, companies stage an experience whenever they engage customers in a personal, memorable way.

Experiences engage, preferably on emotional, physical, intellectual and even spiritual levels; they don't necessarily entertain. And planning those experiences is akin to planning a series of memories. If that doesn't describe funeral planning at its best, I don't know what does.

The Realms of Experience

If experiences aren't about entertaining but engaging, what constitutes a non-entertaining experience? There are four "realms of experience," according to Pine and Gilmore, and entertainment is just one. You can guess what the entertainment realm is all about (think Disney again). The other three are educational, escapist and esthetic.

In the educational realm, people learn as part of their experience. Here at the Center for Loss in Fort Collins, Colorado, I teach a number of week-long courses to bereavement caregivers each year. Groups of 18 caregivers such as hospice workers, clergy, funeral directors, and physicians gather to learn from me and each other. Their experience includes five days of interactive, discussion-based content, as well as sharing their own personal stories of loss, listening to music, enjoying meals together and hiking in the rugged mountain

---

The Four Realms of Experience

Entertainment

Using ideas such as tasteful humor in a eulogy and talented live musicians, and, especially, securing a beautiful, comfortable gathering room that encourages family and friends to linger and enjoy each other's company

Educational

Giving families the opportunity to learn about funerals and why they are important. This can be accomplished by handing out pamphlets or giving talks to community groups.

Escapist

Encouraging families to actively engage in activities during the visitation, funeral and committal. These can range from lighting candles to standing up and sharing memories to laying flowers on the casket.

Esthetic

Creating a positive atmosphere, one that engages all the senses and in which people feel good about spending their time. This can involve good lighting, quality sound and other subtle but extremely important cues.

---

foothills around the Center. The Center itself is a lovely hexagonal-shaped building with many windows, comfortable seating and a tasteful decor.

Consciously, I have set the stage to make this week of education as much of an experience as possible for everyone who participates.

The escapist realm, on the other hand, immerses participants in a totally different reality. Examples of escapist environments include theme parks, chat rooms, laser tag centers and casinos. Have you ever tried to find your way around a mirrored, labyrinthine casino without getting lost or disoriented? Casino designers are very good at creating escapist experiences. Escapist experiences actively involve customers; people come to "do" in the escapist realm.

The escapist realm would ask: What can bereaved families and friends "do" at the visitation or funeral to further immerse themselves in the experience?

In the esthetic realm, people come just to "be." This realm immerses people in unique and often awesome events or environments in a passive way. Relaxing on the ocean shore, viewing the Louvre's Mona Lisa, gazing up at a lunar eclipse, soaking up the atmosphere in Time's Square—these are esthetic experiences.

Funerals traditionally are esthetic experiences. People come to funerals just to "be there," to demonstrate their support and love by their presence. For the most part, they do not play an active role in the funeral itself, but rather "take in" the sights, the sounds, the readings, the music. They allow their thoughts and feelings to wash over them as they focus on the life and death of the person who died.

Esthetic funeral experiences are wonderful and healing, particularly when caregivers do a good job of creating a sense of place, engaging all the senses and eliminating negative cues (distractions such as poor sound quality). However, exceptional funeral planning attempts to integrate more than one realm of experience for bereaved families and friends. The escapist realm, in particular, offers many possibilities for funeral planners; indeed, we are already seeing a trend toward escapist funerals.

The escapist realm would ask: What can bereaved families and friends "do" at the visitation or funeral to further immerse themselves in the experience? When you sit down with families and actively engage them in arranging the funeral, you are creating an escapist experience. When family members and friends participate in the service by giving readings, playing music, sharing memories and lighting candles, they are in escapist realm territory. When funeral guests not only sign the guestbook but are asked to write down a specific memory of the person who died, they are venturing into the escapist realm. When people lay flowers or throw dirt atop the casket at the close of the committal service, they are in the escapist realm of experience. Anything you as a funeral facilitator can do to present families with "escapist" options—never forcing them but encouraging them to take advantage of these healing activities—helps create an exceptional funeral experience.

Are you helping create experiences with a sense of place worthy of a family's time, budget and love for the person who died?

The educational realm is also not out of place in funeral service. I recently created a poster titled "Why We Have Had Funerals Since the Beginning of Time: Wolfelt's Hierarchy of the Purposes of Funerals." On the poster I describe the six purposes of meaningful funeral ceremonies: Reality, Recall, Support, Expression, Meaning, and Transcendence. My goal was to create an accessible and aesthetically pleasing reminder for creating meaningful funeral ceremonies. When meeting with families, you and your staff could glance at the poster and remember your main purpose—your "why"—for creating meaningful funeral ceremonies. It can be used to educate families and to guide decisions on which elements to include to create a valuable funeral experience. (If you are interested, see page 30 for information on ordering the poster.) Giving talks to service clubs and other community organizations about the history and importance of funeral service is yet another way to capitalize on the educational realm.

The entertainment realm of experience can also be used to great effect in funeral planning. While few would term the funeral an "entertaining" experience, humor is certainly an appropriate part of many eulogies. The gathering or reception after the funeral is perhaps the best time to consider the entertainment realm: tasty and visually appetizing foods; memory tables filled with memorabilia that encourages mourners to reminisce about "the good times;" more festive decorating and lighting; round tables surrounded by upholstered chairs. All these things encourage family and friends to stay, to stick around, to talk and enjoy each other's company.

According to Gilmore and Pine, "When all four realms abide within a single setting, then and only then does plain space become a distinctive place for staging an experience. Occurring over a period of time, staged experiences require a sense of place to entice guests to spend more time engaged in the offering."

Are you helping create experiences with a sense of place worthy of a family's time, budget and love for the person who died?

A Sense of Place

In funeral planning, the sense of place has to do with the "where" of the funeral. Will the funeral be held in a church or other place of worship? Will it be held at a funeral home? Or will it be held in another location, perhaps one that holds special meaning for the bereaved family?

When helping a family choose a location for the visitation, the ceremony and the gathering (which sometimes are held at three different places), keep in mind the location's ambiance and emotional qualities. What does the facility look like, inside and out? What message do the décor and the layout send to bereaved families? It is inviting, clean, well kept, easy to move around?

Many companies in the Experience Economy are "theming" their offerings; think of the Rainforest Café, Niketown, and the San Diego Zoo's Wild Animal Park. I bid you to consider the "theme" of the space in which you hold funerals. Is it dark, formal and heavily patterned in its wallpaper and upholstery? Is it nondescript? Is it angular, clean-lined and contemporary? No single environment will suit all bereaved families. But a location that can be somewhat personalized with the person who has died as theme will be the perfect fit for every family who walks through your door.

The person who died as theme? Think of your facility as a blank slate. It's your job to customize the space as much as possible for every new family. Certainly you'll have to choose or work within an existing architectural style. But if you make the spaces beautifully lit, simply decorated—perhaps with plants, wooden furniture, and neutral fabrics—and comfortable, you can then "set the stage" for each unique funeral or visitation.

Did the person who died love lilacs? Fill the visitation room with lilacs. Did the person who died make quilts? Hang her quilts on all the walls and atop the casket. Did the person who died play the bass? Create a display of his beautiful instrument and sheet music, together with photos of him playing the bass. Was the person who died first and foremost a mother? Place the tools of her trade around the room: books she read to her children; toys she lovingly tended for them; photos of her and her children together. I know a funeral home that set the stage for a horse lover who died by placing his casket on top of hay bales and "saddling up" the casket.

At Flanner & Buchanan Mortuaries in Indiana, each family that calls is asked to bring a photograph of the person who died to the arrangement conference. The funeral home has a local media company enlarge the photo to portrait size and places it in a beautiful frame with the name and dates of the person who died. The portrait is set on an easel by the register book and is presented to the family

Creative Locations for Meaningful Funeral Experiences

Jack Bauer of Bauer Funeral Home, Kittanning, Pennsylvania (a small community north of Pittsburgh) was good enough to share these stories with me. In recent years, Bauer Funeral Home orchestrated three particularly interesting funerals in three unique locations.

In the first, Jennifer, a champion figure skater who was a senior in high school, died in a car crash. "When I went to the house to talk with the family, the aunt answered the door and said, 'Now I want you to understand—they don't want a funeral and they don't want to talk to you.'," explains Jack. "Understandably, this family was very upset. With the aunt's help, I was finally able to begin talking with the parents. Jack had been thinking about the fact that this family wasn't attached to a church. What location did hold meaning for them? Since Jennifer was a competitive figure skater, they spent hours and hours every week at the local ice arena. Jack suggested to them that they could hold a service at the ice rink. Within minutes the parents had not only embraced the idea but were coming up with many other ideas of their own.

During the ceremony, 30 skaters from the skating team were seated on the ice. Jennifer's coaches displayed her trophies. Jennifer's mom and dad sat in the bleachers where they always sat to watch Jennifer skate. That arena holds about 700 people and it was filled to capacity.

Jack also held a funeral on a tennis court for an older tennis buff who lived in his community. She played tennis all the time—well into her 80s—and the town named the court on which she played Maude Maize Tennis Court. When she died, Jack called her relatives, who lived out of state. She had no children, just nieces and nephews, and they requested direct cremation. But Jack and the family agreed that in the spring, they would hold a memorial service for Maude. So when the weather started getting nicer, he called them back and suggested they hold her service on her tennis court. The family loved the idea. They created a simple ceremony in memory of Maude.

"With about 40 of us seated on the tennis court," Jack explains, "they read scripture and shared stories for an hour and a half. They also released helium balloons. Then we served punch and cookies right there. It was so fitting."

The third unique service location Jack hit upon was the country club. A local doctor's wife had died. He said he was an atheist and that he wanted direct cremation. Jack persuaded him that since he and his wife, Brownie, had so many friends in this community and had lived there for so long, he should have some sort of gathering in her honor. Finally they decided on a reception to be held two days later at the country club. Jack also asked the doctor to bring him 25-30 photos of Brownie from throughout her life for a video memorial tribute.

"My daughter and I put together an order of service for the reception," says Jack. "We told some stories about her and invited others to do the same. Then we showed the video and darned if the doctor didn't stand up and start narrating Brownie's life story. He talked about each photo of her as it appeared on the screen. And then he proceeded to lead the rest of the service himself. At the end of the service, we all toasted Brownie while singing 'Auld Lang Syne.'"

Congratulations, Jack, on having helped create three meaningful experiences where there might have been none at all. In each of these three cases, suggesting a different locale opened the door to a whole new world of ideas for these families.

---

after services. A little touch, yes, but one that has made a much better experience for Flanner & Buchanan customers.

Of course, the funeral home isn't the only place to hold visitations or funerals. In addition to churches or other places of worship, funerals can be held almost anywhere: barns, meadows, golf courses, riverbanks. If the person who died were the theme, where would be the most meaningful place to hold the ceremony? Somewhere meaningful to the person who died or to her family. This is often particularly appropriate for non-religious families, but even deeply religious services can be held in atypical locations if the family and the funeral officiant are so inclined. If you open your heart and mind to this concept, you'll see that funerals and memorial services can be held almost anywhere—parks, football fields, homes, riverbanks, horse barns. Almost any place that holds special meaning for the family and friends of the person who died is appropriate.

Now's also a good time to emphasize the importance and versatility of photos in creating a sense of place and, ultimately, an exceptional funeral experience. Many funeral planners encourage families to create memory boards or bring in a framed photo or two to display. But if you're truly setting the stage, it's your job as funeral facilitator to help families creatively and effectively display photos. Yes, I agree that it's healing for family members themselves to gather and organize photos for a memory board or display. But there's so much more that can be done with those same photos! Beacham McDougald Funeral Home and Crematorium in North Carolina routinely creates "Life Reflections" photo shows that are displayed on a 36" color TV at the visitation. You can also buy large format printers that will print oversized images of photos you've scanned in. Imagine several poster-size photos of the person who died, placed in simple poster frames and hung on the visitation room or chapel walls instead of blah prints or paintings. Do you have display easels or stands for photo albums? Do you have the means to edit home videos and play them at the funeral? Do you use scanned photos of the person who died in personalized programs? Does your website post obituaries and online "guestbooks"?

Personalizing the visitation, funeral and gathering spaces in honor of the person who died helps create an experience that's about the person who died and the people who loved him. It further immerses families in the esthetic and escapist realms. It encourages them to stay, to spend time together, in contemplation and honor of the unique person who died.

Engage the Five Senses

At the beginning of this section I asked you to think about a particularly memorable experience. Chances are you can remember many sensory details, including sights, sounds, tastes, textures, and smells. In fact, the more an experience engages all five senses, the more memorable it is.

For funerals, you might consider the impact of the following sensory input on the overall experience:

Sense	Cues
Sight	Facility décor, lighting, colors, the body, memorabilia displays and other elements of personalization, cleanliness
Sound	Music, readings, squeaky doors or floorboards, sound system quality, acoustics, background noises (heating, air conditioning, nearby traffic, etc.)
Touch	Upholstery, seating comfort, the body, the casket, touchable memorabilia displays, the program
Smell	Flowers, embalming/chemical smells, food
Taste	At reception: food quality, selection, tastiness; mints, drinks or other refreshments that guests are offered

How can you improve or enhance the ways in which you engage families' senses? One relatively inexpensive and simple way that comes to mind is lighting. I think that lighting for a funeral should be warm and bright but not harsh. Well-placed cans or hanging fixtures can create an inviting mood for display tables and conversation areas. Consider adding windows to dark rooms or revamping window treatments to allow for better lighting. How is the lighting in your facility? What mood does it create? Bring in a talented lighting designer and see what she thinks.

Personalizing the visitation, funeral and gathering spaces in honor of the person who died helps create an experience that's about the person who died and the people who loved him.

Sound system quality is another important sensory cue. Have you ever listened to music on really good, really well placed speakers? It's like the difference between flying first class and flying in the cargo hold. Music helps mourners embrace their feelings. It immerses them in the experience. Poor sound quality, feedback and other audio problems jolt them out of the experience. Investing in good sound equipment (and video equipment, too) is definitely one of the most important investments you can make.

It's easy to overlook the sense of smell in funeral planning. The field of aromatherapy has many ideas to offer. Scented candles might be just right for some visitations or funerals (think vanilla for someone who liked to bake or pine for an outdoorsperson). Aroma oils in scents of lavender or citrus or mint could add a nice touch. Flowers with distinctive smells are always appropriate. Like too much perfume, too much scent or too many competing scents are bad ideas. But used sparingly and chosen with care based on the likes and dislikes of the person who died and her family, scent can make an experience come alive and awaken poignant memories.

I'm sure you can think of many more ways to engage all five senses during the meaningful funeral if you think creatively and with an open mind. I do understand that some of the sensory input discussed in this section will be beyond your control. Still, it is important to consider. Whatever you do, don't discount this subtle but critical facet of creating exceptional funeral experiences.

A Final Word About Experiences

Now that you've begun to think about funerals as experiences—experiences to which you hold the key, I'll bet you can think of all kinds of ideas for enhancing the funeral experience for the families in your care. The options are literally endless. All it takes is a little creative thinking and a passion to help mourners begin to heal through the power of personalized ceremony.

How will you help the next bereaved family that walks through your door? Will you fall back on the old "here's how it's done" approach, with you as functionary instead of facilitator? Or will you make an effort to first get to know this unique family and the love they have for the person who died, and then help them create an equally unique funeral experience worthy of that love?

Remember that you have the power to change lives. You hold the key to the transformative funeral experience. Use it well.

The Caregiver's Role in Creating Meaningful Funeral Ceremonies

"The one who conducts the funeral . . . must have a capacity for empathy, understanding of the situation of mourners and knowing something of what they are feeling. He (or she) must be ready to accept the mourners as they are, not trying to press upon them attitudes or patterns of behavior that are not genuinely their own. . . Since no two situations are identical, there must be sufficient flexibility in the funeral to make it relevant and meaningful in each situation."
– Paul Irion

What makes an effective funeral officiant? This is not a simple question to answer, for effective officiants have philosophies and "ways of being" as varied as those of the people they help.

Historically, funeral officiants have been clergy. Indeed, I expect that many of the caregivers who will read this book, particularly this section, will be members of the clergy. To you I offer my professional thanks and respect for having for so many years upheld the tradition of the funeral; I hope the contents herein will challenge and renew your commitment to meaningfulness in the funeral ceremonies you officiate.

As society has become increasingly secular, however, a growing trend toward the use of laypeople—family members, friends of the family, funeral directors, attorneys—as funeral facilitators or "celebrants" has emerged. (More and more funeral homes across North America are training funeral directors to act as "ritual specialists" for families with no religious affiliation.) I welcome you, too, to this discussion. In fact, I believe that those families who come to the funeral process without religious ties are often better helped by secular officiants. Regardless of your background, if you are interested in helping the newly bereaved by planning and/or facilitating a funeral, I invite your consideration of this material.

You will note the use of the historical term *funeral officiant* as well as the more modern *funeral facilitator* throughout Parts 4 and 5 of this book. The latter term may sound strange to traditionally-trained ears, but I use it purposefully to invite new ways of thinking about funerals. To facilitate literally means "to make easier," and as I will discuss in this section, one of the most important roles of the funeral officiant is to ease and optimize the bereaved family's early grief. The word facilitator also implies openness and helpfulness, while officiant can smack of formality and hierarchical superiority—connotations that run counter to the model of funeral caregiving I support. Finally, a facilitator might be an uncle, a college buddy or an attorney, while an officiant is almost always a member of the clergy. To recognize both groups as funereal caregivers I use both terms.

Having said that defining an effective funeral facilitator is difficult, I must also say this: In my many years as a grief counselor and death educator, I have met some wonderful and some not so wonderful funeral facilitators and I have drawn some broadstroke conclusions about both groups. In this section I will explore the qualities that, based on my observations, effective funeral facilitators share.

Spend a few minutes thinking about the qualities you have found most helpful in your work with newly bereaved families. Think about your strengths as well as those of other funeral facilitators you know, then jot down your thoughts here:

____

____

____

____

____

____

____

____

____

____

____

____

____

____

When you've finished reading this text section, come back to this box and see if you can brainstorm any additional helpful caregiver qualities.

"One friend, one person who is truly understanding, who takes the trouble to listen to us as we consider our problems, can change our whole outlook on the world."
– Dr. Elliott Mayo

The qualities of the effective funeral facilitator

Here's my list, which I have designed to double as a self-assessment tool. As you read through it, I invite you to rate your skills in each area on a scale of 1 (low) to 5 (high). Be honest as you consider both your strengths and your weaknesses. For a more objective assessment, you might also have a friend or colleague rate your skills.

1. **The willingness to adopt a "teach me" attitude.**
   Effective funeral facilitators are always learning from those they help. In fact, they realize that bereaved families are the only ones who can teach them about their unique experiences and needs. An effective funeral facilitator sits down with the newly bereaved family and, through a combination of listening and gentle guiding, in effect says, "Teach me what this death has been like for you. Teach me how I can best help you plan and carry out a meaningful funeral ceremony." This "teach me" attitude lets bereaved families know that above all else, you respect their thoughts and feelings.

   For experienced funeral facilitators, this means setting aside your preconceptions and your "standard" practices. Instead, I challenge you to view each new family in a special light. What are the unique needs of this family? Is a traditional service appropriate for them? If not, what might be? This "clean slate" approach can be draining and time-consuming, I admit, but rigid, cookie-cutter ceremonies are little better than no ceremony at all.

Low Average High

1 2 3 4 5

"They sat with Job on the ground seven days and seven nights. No one spoke a word to him for they saw how very great he was suffering."
– Job 3:13

2. **The desire and ability to connect with the bereaved family.**
   The effective funeral facilitator takes the time and expends the energy to connect to the newly bereaved family before the service. Too often I have witnessed the fast food approach to funeral planning: the funeral director makes the call to the funeral facilitator, often a clergy member, who then pencils in the time and date on his or her calendar. Little (sometimes none at all) contact is made with the bereaved family before the funeral. At the ceremony, the officiant pulls out his or her standard service, sprinkling the dead person's name and a few life details here and there. The bereaved family and friends leave the service as numb as when they arrived.

Effective funerals are personalized (more about that in the last section of this resource.) And effective funereal caregiving is personalized, too. You cannot help the newly bereaved family plan a meaningful funeral unless you are physically, emotionally and spiritually present for them in their time of need.

Low Average High

1 2 3 4 5

3. The capacity for empathy.

Effective funeral facilitators are empathetic. This means you must develop the capacity to project yourself into the bereaved family's world and to be involved in the emotional suffering inherent in the work of grief. You must strive to understand the meaning of the family's experience instead of imposing meaning on that experience from the outside.

Listening, actively listening, is a critical part of empathy. Actually, listening is a critical component of all the qualities I have listed here. If you listen, the families you serve will tell you—through their words, their gestures, their presence—how you can best help them during this extraordinarily difficult time.

Low Average High

1 2 3 4 5

"When somebody's presence does really make itself felt, it can refresh my inner being; it reveals me to myself, it makes me feel more fully myself than I should be if I were not exposed to its impact."

– Gabriel Marcel

4. The capacity for warmth and caring.

To be an effective funeral facilitator, you must strive for a sense of personal closeness, not professional distance, with the families you help. Though they will not often tell you this, they will be thinking, "Before I care about how much you know, I need to know about how much you care."

Warmth is primarily communicated nonverbally, through facial expressions, posture, gesture and touch. Yes, even touch. While you must assess each individual family's need for and openness to touch, you must also offer your touch when that need makes itself apparent. Remember, however, that touch is culture- and relationship-dependent and that before you can offer physical comfort, you must first establish a relationship with the bereaved family.

As a bereavement caregiver, you have an opportunity—a responsibility—to comfort grieving families and to be emotionally available to them.

Low Average High

1 2 3 4 5

Listening

Really listening to families as you help them plan and carry out meaningful funeral experiences may be the most important skill you bring to the process. You must demonstrate a desire to understand and be responsive to their unique needs. You must be aware of both verbal and non-verbal signals they give you. You must find out not only what the family wants and needs to make for a meaningful funeral experience, but what they don't want. One great way to determine what families may want and don't want is to ask them, "Have you ever seen something done at a funeral that you really liked? Disliked?"

Like the most sensitive receptors, you must be on what some people call "high receive." Even the quiet remark made by someone during your initial meeting may offer clues to a way you can bring meaning to the funeral experience.

Ask questions that assist you in your efforts to understand. Listen carefully and with attention to detail. Don't mentally wander, even when someone is talking about something you may already know (e.g. the cause of the death, which clergy person will facilitate the ceremony, or what cemetery will be used). Don't interrupt when others are talking. Allow, even encourage, times of silence for people to gather their thoughts. Give your undivided attention.

Personal Qualities of An Effective Listener

Desire. Perhaps the single most important characteristic of the good listener is desire. While this sounds simplistic, you need to want to listen. Remember—people can quickly detect a superficial desire to listen.

Commitment. An effective listener not only needs to have a general desire to listen, but also needs to be committed to the task of listening. To be committed means to be responsible. If you are unable to talk at a particular time, be honest. Share your desire to talk and arrange for another time.

Patience. In addition to desire and commitment, the listening funeral planner needs to have patience. If you are in a hurry and are anxious to get the situation "taken care of," chances are that you will do a poor job of listening. Be patient and available to provide the understanding bereaved families seek from you.

Another facet of listening patience is learning that you do not need to fill every silence. There is a time for speaking and a time for silence. Sometimes in your effort to help, you may feel the need to keep the conversation going. Discipline yourself and remember: Listening also involves listening to the silent moments as the other person struggles to express a feeling or pauses to consider a thought.

Attending—Listening's Cohort

Listening with your ears is just one part of truly listening. Listening with your body, or what I call attending, further communicates your desire to help bereaved families. Body language such as eye contact, posture, physical distance, facial expression, gesture, tone of voice, rate of speech, and energy level all communicate something about your ability to listen. Even seemingly superficial characteristics such as physical appearance and setting make a difference.

When you learn that more than two-thirds of all communication takes place through non-verbal means, you can understand the importance of developing attending skills.

Eye contact. Perhaps the most effective way of making contact with people, especially shortly after a death, is to look them in the eye as you talk with them. While you certainly do not have to maintain a fixed stare, the appropriate procedure is to look at the people you are helping both while they are talking with you and during times of silence. Also, don't ignore people who by their nature or current emotional state are very quiet. You still want to make eye contact with them to help them feel included and supported. Of course, eye contact means different things to people of different cultures. Keep this important caveat in mind as you as you work with families of various cultural backgrounds.

Posture. A second component of attending is posture. Each moment of every day, we communicate a great deal by how we stand, sit and walk. Take a moment right now to become aware of your posture and what it might communicate to someone entering the room. Interested listeners lean into a conversation and are relaxed in posture; disinterested or unfriendly listeners lean away from the speaker and fold their arms across their chests. Can you picture the difference?

Physical distance. In general, physical closeness demonstrates a desire to help. Use the bereaved person's reaction as a guide. If he or she draws back, take that as an indication that you are too close. We have found that most people are comfortable talking at a distance of about three feet. Try to arrange seating to take advantage of this.

Facial expression. The expression on your face should match, as closely as possible, the emotional tone of what is occurring around you. Few people are more aware of the importance of this than those involved in funeral service. Your facial expressions can easily communicate a sense of warmth, as well as the message, "I am with you, I understand, and I want to help you." You may find that you communicate something differently with your facial expression than you are aware. After all, to see your facial expression is difficult unless you look in a mirror. You might want to ask your family, friends, and co-workers how they perceive your different expressions.

Gesture. You communicate much not only through your posture, but through your body movements. Your gestures should be natural and not interfere with your intended communication. If you move quickly or have mannerisms that are distracting, you will take a great deal away from your ability to help. Ask yourself if your gestures communicate what you are trying to communicate.

Poor attending behaviors tend to stop conversation or prohibit a helping relationship from being established. If you find yourself unable to pay attention effectively over a period of time, you will most likely notice some changes in the family's behavior. They may become passive and have difficulty in sharing their hurt in a mutual relationship. The result is that you'll probably move into a question/answer pattern difficult to get out of. On the other hand, they may become upset, impatient, and angry because you do not appear interested and concerned. These are signs that your attending skills are lacking and indicate that the person is not satisfied with the level of attention you are offering.

---

5. An understanding of your professional and personal self.

Effective funeral facilitators understand that their past professional and private experiences with not just funerals but with grief in general affect their work. Actually, you bring the sum total of all your life's experiences to each family you help. You must strive to understand how your background, your strengths and weaknesses, your personal biases—your ways of being—color each funeral you facilitate.

Self-awareness is critical to the helping process. I truly believe that you cannot fully understand others unless you have first made the effort to fully understand yourself. Remind yourself each time you sit down with a newly bereaved family that your primary responsibility is to identify their needs and wants and then to help them carry out those needs and wants in the form of a meaningful funeral ceremony. Meaningful for *them*. They need your compassion and gentle guidance, not your insistence on a particular course of action.

Low Average High

1 2 3 4 5

6. The willingness to develop a personal theory of funeral facilitation.

As a funeral facilitator, you believe your work is important. But it may have been years since you have been asked to articulate why.

Why do you believe funerals are important? What, specifically, constitutes a meaningful funeral ceremony? What do you see as your role in helping bereaved families with the funeral? These are the sorts of questions that, when answered, might go into your own personal philosophy of funerals. While we can borrow and build on the ideas of others, there is tremendous value in challenging ourselves to articulate our own key assumptions about the helping process.

Low Average High

1 2 3 4 5

"One of the startling discoveries of my life was when I noticed how trained I was to talk and how untrained I was to listen."
– Pastor Doug Manning

Your personal funeral philosophy

Here are a few blank lines for you take notes about your personal funeral philosophy. I encourage you to later refine those notes into a formal, written statement that can guide you in your funeral work.

____

____

____

____

____

7. The desire to seek new knowledge about grief and effective funeral facilitation.

To continue to be effective, the bereavement caregiver must be committed to ongoing education. You must take advantage of new resources and training opportunities as they become available. The key, of course, is then to take your new insights and learn to apply them in your work with newly bereaved families.

Experienced funeral facilitators also have an opportunity to educate others about the funeral ritual. Perhaps your colleagues would benefit from a regular roundtable discussion of their funeral work. Or surely your church or community group would be interested in a talk on some of the topics in this booklet. Challenge yourself to plan these types of knowledge-sharing. Of course, each time you meet a new bereaved family you have a responsibility to teach them about the importance of meaningful funeral rituals. This does not mean you must dictate what is best for them, but that you must provide them with the information they need to make sound decisions for themselves.

Low Average High

1 2 3 4 5

8. The capacity to feel personally adequate and to have self-respect.

Helpful bereavement caregivers feel good about themselves. They feel good about their ability to relate to newly bereaved families. Their sense of self-value invites the same self-assuredness in the families they help.

PLEASE DON'T

Don'ts for funeral facilitators

Don't be a functionary.
Be a facilitator. Think of creating funerals not as a chore but as your most important challenge.

Don't prescribe.
Gently guide, instead. Avoid telling families what they must do or not do as part of their funeral.

Don't be rigid.
Be flexible. Don't out-of-hand reject a special request just because it's "not been done before." Try to be flexible as you help each unique family.

Don't be defensive.
Be understanding. The time immediately after a death is difficult for everyone involved. You are the figure most prominent during this time and as such can become a "whipping post" for the family's anger, fears and frustration. Try not to take it personally.

Don't forget about the family.
Stay in touch. Bereaved families often complain to me that once the funeral is over, they never hear from the funeral officiant again. Families feel abandoned when this happens.

Don't under-commit.
Spend some time with the family. Don't think you can create a meaningful funeral ceremony without first spending some time to get to know the family involved. You must create an alliance with the bereaved.

Don't over-commit.
Know your limits. While you play a crucial role in helping families create meaningful funeral ceremonies, you can't be a superperson. Don't overextend yourself. Take the time to relax and reinvigorate. Ask for help.

"Comforting the mourner is an act of loving-kindness toward both the living and the dead."
– Kitzur Shulkhan Arukh 193:11

Effective funeral facilitators never feel superior to those they help, however. They offer their knowledge and experience freely, gladly. They do not talk down to bereaved families and they do not let their time constraints make the families feel they are being rushed or neglected.

Low Average High

1 2 3 4 5

9. The ability to recognize and accept one's personal power in the helping relationship.

Tremendous responsibility comes with the helping relationship you have been entrusted with. Because support is so often lacking elsewhere, bereaved families will rely on you—sometimes you alone—to help them through their early weeks of grief. Do not be frightened by this temporary, heightened dependence on you.

But do not misuse this power, either. You should not feel superior to the families you work with but instead realize that your helping role is to empower them by encouraging their own autonomy and discovery of strengths. Paradoxically, keeping your own personal power under control stimulates the personal power of the bereaved family.

Low Average High

1 2 3 4 5

10. The desire for continued growth, both personally and professionally.

Effective bereavement caregivers continually assess their strengths and weaknesses. They stay in touch with their own losses and how those losses influence and change their lives. In the same way that they encourage the families they work with to grow, they strive to clarify their own values and live by them rather than by the expectations of those around them. They yearn to continue to live and grow each day.

Low Average High

1 2 3 4 5

So, how did you do? While there is no acceptable or unacceptable overall "score," I suggest that you examine those areas for which you circled a 1, 2 or even a 3. This is not to say that to be considered good at what you do, you as a funeral facilitator must "score" high in all the above areas. Instead, I urge you to use this list as a personal and professional challenge. Ask yourself, first of all, if you agree that the qualities I have enumerated are useful to effective funeral facilitation. You might then set a specific course of action for improving your skills where they are weak.

After six months or a year has passed, rerate yourself to check for improvement. If you take this self-assessment seriously, you may find it will help you gain insight into your work with bereaved families, enriching your career and perhaps most important, heightening the profound, healing benefits of a meaningful funeral ceremony for the bereaved people in your care.

Helping the newly bereaved is one of the most draining tasks on earth. But as many of you know, it can offer unparalleled satisfaction. It follows, then, that while becoming a better helper to the newly bereaved is hard work, it, too, is well worth the effort. I challenge you to challenge yourselves and to hone those qualities that make you a better caregiver.

"Guard your inner spirit more than any treasure, for it is the source of life."
– An ancient sage

The Funeral Facilitator's Most Important Tasks

1. Listening
   As I have said, empathetic listening is the essential helping skill. When you take the time to listen to newly bereaved families, you are letting them know that you do not have all the answers and that you need to hear their thoughts and feelings if you are to help them plan a funeral that will be meaningful to them.

2. Understanding
   To understand the bereaved means to be familiar with those thoughts, feelings and behaviors common to the experience of grief, especially in the first few days following a death. You must adopt a "teach me" attitude if you are to truly understand each bereaved family's needs.

3. Educating
   While a "teach me" attitude is essential to bereavement caregivers, so is the ability to educate bereaved families about the experience of grief and the funeral's role in beginning to assuage that grief. Guide them through the funeral process—something they may have little or no experience with.

4. Supporting
   If you are to help bereaved families heal, you must help support them not just through the funeral, but through the healthy reconciliation of their grief—a process which may take years. Be available to them before, during and after the funeral.

5. Advocating
   At times the funeral facilitator may need to advocate for the bereaved family. For example, you may need to intervene when a well-intentioned but misinformed friend encourages the family not to have a funeral. More generally, advocating for the bereaved means providing a safe atmosphere in which bereaved people feel safe to express themselves.

6. Encouraging
   The family who comes to you for help with funeral planning may think their acute grief will never subside. While you should be realistic about the ongoing pain they will likely encounter, you must also offer them hope for healing. Let them know that these first days and weeks after the death are among the most difficult and that with time and the gentle understanding of those around them, they can and will learn to reconcile their grief and go on to find continued meaning in life and living.

7. Referring
   Funeral facilitators cannot be and should not be a bereaved family's only helping resource. While you need to put forth the time and energy to create a meaningful funeral and to follow up with the family in the weeks and months after the funeral, you must also realize your own limitations and refer the family to community resources for extra help. You are responsible *to* families, not *for* them.

Practical Ideas for Creating Meaningful Funerals

PART 5

"It is crucial to be aware of the spiritual crisis on our planet ... The unprecedented speed of social change has produced a massive collapse of the traditional system of religious beliefs, symbols, meanings and values for millions on planet earth. Traditional authority-centered ways of handling existential anxiety and satisfying spiritual needs are no longer acceptable or meaningful to them. But they have not yet developed new, more creative ways."
– Howard Clinebell

Funerals are most meaningful when they are personalized tributes to the unique life and relationships of the person who died.

This is not to say that standard funeral services should not be used. Indeed, we have already acknowledged that established rituals often comfort participants. Traditional religious funeral ceremonies, especially, can provide a sense of meaningful structure and continuity. Indeed, the importance—historically and presently—of faith in the funeral ritual cannot be understated. Over the course of human history, most funeral ceremonies have been products of humankind's religious beliefs. The funeral, perhaps like no other event, calls into question the very meaning of life and death. So, each faith group has naturally created a funeral ceremony reflecting its beliefs about life and death and providing answers to our most profound questions: Why are we put on this earth? Why must we die? Is there life after death? For these reasons, religious funerals can be the most meaningful—at least to believers.

Traditional religious funeral ceremonies, especially, can provide a sense of meaningful structure and continuity.

Many of you reading this book are members of the clergy and as such have given your lives to the beliefs upheld by your faith's funeral ceremonies. I respect your traditional, sanctioned ceremonies and am not asking you to abandon them. But I do believe that standard funeral services, no matter how spiritually resonant, do not fully meet the needs of the bereaved unless the service also captures the uniqueness of the person who died. I am asking you to think of the ceremonies set forth in your books of worship as foundations on which a truly meaningful funeral for a particular family can be constructed. In other words, funerals should be personalized tributes to the person who died.

That bears repeating.

Some Ideas to Offer to Families in Helping Them Personalize a Funeral Service

As you are meeting with the family, emphasize that the funeral service they have should be as special as the life they will be remembering. Here are a few ideas:

- Write a personalized obituary. Some newspapers allow you to express a little more than the usual who/what/why/where/when. Appoint a creative "word" person in the family to handle this task.
- Create a column in the guest book for people to jot down a memory after they sign their name.
- Display personal items or hobby paraphernalia on a table at the visitation, the ceremony and/or the gathering afterwards.
- Have more than one person deliver the eulogy. Ask several people to share memories and talk about different aspects of the person who died.
- Choose clothing for the person who died that reflects his or her life, interests, passions, etc. The clothing needn't be formal or somber!
- Create a personalized program for the ceremony. You can include photos, poems, anecdotes—whatever you'd like!
- Show a videotape or slide show of the person's life during the funeral. Pictures tell a thousand words!
- Ask children if they would like to write a letter or draw a picture for the person who died. Their "goodbyes" can then be placed in the casket alongside the body.
- Select flowers that were meaningful to the person who died. A simple arrangement of freshly cut lilacs, for example, might be perfect.
- At the funeral, invite people to write down a memory of the person who died. Appoint someone to gather and read the memories aloud.
- Create a funeral that captures the personality of the person who died. If he was zany, don't be afraid to use humor. If she was affectionate, have everyone stand up and hug the person next to them during the ceremony.
- Display photos of the person who died at the visitation, the ceremony and/or the gathering. In fact, putting together a photo collage can be a very healing experience for the family in the days before the funeral.
- Use a lot of music, especially if music was meaningful to the person who died or is to the family. Music can be played at the visitation, the committal service and the gathering as well as the funeral service itself!
- Create a personalized grave marker. Include a poem, a drawing or a short phrase that defines the person who died.

Funerals should be personalized tributes to the person who died.

One crucial part of your job is to help families think about the qualities of the person who died and what this person meant to others and then USE this information to create a personalized ceremony. Consider his or her passions, hobbies, pastimes, likes, dislikes. How can you help this family capture this unique life?

Be creative as you, together with the family and others who will participate in the service, brainstorm how to remember and honor the person who died.

John Kane of R.S. Kane Funeral Home in Ontario related several ideas he has used for personalizing the service. For one funeral, the son mentioned that his father had been in the 48th Highlanders Regiment. Together they decided that a bagpiper would be appropriate and that the father's jacket, which had very special buttons, should be on display in the visitation room rather than the casket as first planned. For an ardent golfer, the funeral home's floral designer was given the golf bag to use as a "vase." This arrangement was placed at the head of the casket. For a young man who loved his red, custom-built car, the funeral director suggested parking the car near the funeral home's front door on the day of the service. The engine was revved as people left. John himself led the funeral procession on his Harley for a friend's funeral.

How can you help this family capture this unique life?

If you truly listen to families and are genuinely interested in learning about the person who died, they will tell you what you need to know to help them personalize the service. Pick up on their cues and make creative suggestions.

In this last section I will offer practical suggestions for funeral planning by revisiting the six reconciliation needs of mourning and the various ways in which these needs can be met by the typical components of a funeral ceremony.

Wait a minute, you might say; there is no such thing as a typical funeral ceremony! It's true that funeral rituals can differ radically from culture to culture and faith to faith. Roman Catholics use a relatively formal ceremony that includes a vigil, a funeral Mass and the committal. The funeral itself consists of prayers, Bible readings, a homily, the liturgy of the Eucharist, communion and the closing rite of commendation. Orthodox Jewish funerals are characterized by expediency and simplicity; ideally the dead person's body (which must not be "viewed") is washed, dressed in white and buried before nightfall or at least within 24 hours of death. And in traditional Hindu funeral services, the family carries the dead body to the cremation chamber and lights the fire.

Still, North American funeral ceremonies, even among various faiths and cultures, include many of the same elements. Often they begin with a **visitation,** which is a time for mourners to view the dead body. Anywhere from several days to several minutes after the visitation, the funeral service itself begins, typically consisting of the **opening**, **readings**, **music**, the **eulogy** and a **closing**. Often following the funeral service is a procession to the cemetery and a short **committal** service. The funeral typically ends with mourners **gathering** together to share a meal and talk.

These are the common elements of funeral ceremony for which I will offer practical "reconciliation" suggestions. If the faith or belief system to which you belong has different funeral elements, I encourage you to examine them, as well, in light of the discussion that follows.

Planning the Ceremony

As I have emphasized already, helping the family plan a meaningful funeral is one of your most important tasks as funeral facilitator. Not only will a thorough planning session (or sessions) ensure a well-thought-out funeral, it will also help the newly bereaved family begin to meet some of the six reconciliation needs of mourning.

Simply by meeting with you and telling you about the life and death of the person who died, for example, the family is acknowledging the reality of the death. Another important "grief moment" during the planning phase occurs when families visit the funeral home to choose a casket. In my experience, this is one of the biggest moments of reality confrontation for mourners. Picking out clothes for the dead person is another.

When you first meet with bereaved families to plan the funeral, an excellent open-ended question to ask is, "What have you seen or experienced at funeral ceremonies that you liked? What didn't you like?" This gives them a chance to articulate their personal tastes before you offer your recommendations.

And remember that the average North American family plans a funeral only once every 20 years. They may be unaware of their choices and their very role in planning the ceremony. Educate them about the importance of meaningful funeral ceremonies while remaining sensitive to their unique needs.

As you read through the following practical funeral suggestions, think about the creative ways in which you might help families meet their six reconciliation needs of mourning. I've left room for your entries next to mine.

You'll note that there is some overlapping among the six needs and that any given moment in the ceremony, whether it be during a reading or music or the eulogy, will often help mourners meet more than one reconciliation need at a time. I do not mean to imply that grief is a series of discrete emotional, cognitive and spiritual tasks.

However, I do hope the pages that follow, in addition to offering you some new suggestions for funeral planning, will help you begin to place a heightened emphasis on meeting the grief needs of mourners during the funerals you officiate.

Visitation

The visitation (also called the wake or calling hours) is an historically rooted practice that unfortunately is being used less and less today. While it is not an element of the funeral that you as a funeral facilitator may have helped "plan," you do have a responsibility to educate bereaved families about the benefits of visitation and suggest some of the following ways to make it more meaningful for them. When at all possible, I also encourage you to attend the visitation yourself, no matter how briefly. Your presence will be seen as a supportive gesture and a confirmation of the family's choice to have a visitation.

Mourning need	Ways to meet this need	Your ideas
1. Acknowledge the reality. of the death.	Simply having a visitation does much to help survivors begin to meet this need. Encourage mourners, including children, to attend.	
2. Move toward the pain of the loss.	Again, seeing the dead body may be in and of itself one of the most therapeutically painful yet important moments for survivors. Help them expect this. You may want to accopany the family into the room for the initial viewing, then give them the personal space and privacy they need. They will often remember you were there with them at this time. Suggest to families that they spend some private time with the body prior to the public visitation.	
3. Remember the person who died.	Because of its relatively loose structure, the visitation often finds mourners talking in small groups about the person who died.	

The registration book is often the first thing families look over after the viewing; make it more meaningful by leaving a column for special memories: "I remember when Bob..." Music that reflects the life of the dead person may be played in the background.

With the family's permission, suggest that people put something special to them in the casket alongside the body. Children especially find this meaningful and may want to color a picture just for this purpose. Mourners of any age may want to write a letter, seal it and place it in the casket.

Talk to mourners about their memories in preparation for your eulogy.

Suggest the family create a memory table on which they display objects that link them to the person who died. Memory boards, on which people pin up a favorite memory of the person who died, are also popular.

4. Develop a new self-identity.

The visitation is an initial dose of self-identity change. Simply by attending, mourners are coming together in a social situation for the first time to support the

	primary mourners in their new roles.	
5. Search for meaning.	Encourage family members to spend some time with the body as they begin to think through their "meaning of life" questions.	
	Use a "Comforting the Bereaved" liturgy containing prayers, memories and psalms at the close of the visitation. Your words can then be used as a prelude to the funeral ceremony the next day.	
6. Receive support from others.	Encourage families to place an obituary and/or funeral notice in the local newspaper, even when it is a paid announcement. The support they may receive in return is well worth it.	
	Educate the family about the supportive messages conveyed by the sending of flowers and the bringing of food.	
	Model support by attending the visitation yourself. Remember to sign the registration book, for you will play a major part in the family history surrounding the death.	

Making Visitation More Meaningful

According to the 2010 FAMIC study of American Attitudes Toward Ritualization and Memorialization, only 5% of people who had attended a funeral service indicated they disliked an open casket. According to the study, nearly three-fourths of Americans choose to have an open casket. That's great news! After all, as you well know, viewing and spending time with the body is a critical step toward reconciling loss for many mourners. (As you also know, however, cremation-only customers are less likely to ask for visitation. The 2010 FAMIC study found that 40% of Americans would not have the cremated body available for viewing at all, 31% would have an open casket prior to cremation, and 23% would have the urn present.

Now consider a past survey conducted by an association of independent family funeral homes, which found that 85% of the respondents say that the opportunity to personalize their own or a loved one's funeral is very important. Boomers and X- and Y-geners don't value generic, cookie-cutter funerals; they want truly unique services that befit the unique life of the person who died.

So, most Americans still want visitation. They also want personalization. How can you combine the two in a powerful, cost-effective way that helps families heal? Many of you have routinely begun using memory boards at visitations. Some of you have also used memorabilia tables or displays, showcasing hobby items or other effects of the person who died. These are both excellent, virtually effortless ways to make the visitation more of a meaningful experience.

Other ideas for enhancing the visitation experience include:

- Filling the visitation room not with traditional funeral flower arrangements but with vase upon vase of the favorite flower of the person who died.
- Dressing the person who died in his favorite clothing or uniform—not formal wear.
- Suggesting that the family help dress the person who died.
- Playing music that is personally meaningful to the family, or favorite music of the person who died, in the background.
- Holding the visitation somewhere special to the family, perhaps the family garden or the beach. (Of course, you'll have to look into permits and consider other issues for public places.)
- Displaying poster-sized photos of the person who died.
- Playing DVD footage of the person's life or running audiotape in the background.

- Setting up a children's corner in the visitation room with quiet toys, books, and paper and crayons and washable markers so children can, if they wish, create drawings and write messages to place inside the casket.

In talking with Beacham McDougald, a funeral director and good friend of mine from McDougald Funeral Home and Crematorium in Laurinburg, North Carolina, I learned of another surprisingly simple yet highly effective way to personalize the visitation with regular photos. He calls them "Life Reflections" shows and you can create them yourself quite easily with a PC, a scanner, and a CD burner.

His "Life Reflections" are simply a collection of photos depicting the life and loves of the person who died. Using a scanner and a piece of software called Corell Presentations, he scans in photos the family brings to him then arranges them in a logical sequence. He runs the Presentation software on a laptop computer which is in turn hooked up to a 36" color TV in a tasteful cabinet (they call it the Presentation Center). The photos are consecutively displayed on the TV screen in a continuous loop throughout the visitation.

Beacham said that he can also integrate text into the presentations. He can caption the photos or intersperse quotes or other text among the photos. His CD burner also came with software that allows him to create custom CD case covers with a photo, name, birth and death dates of the deceased as well as a label for the CD itself.

But here's the really important question: What do families think of the Life Reflections presentations?

In 2002, only 10-20% of the families we serve accepted our offer to do the Life Reflections show for them, even though we don't charge an additional fee," says Beacham. "In 2003 that number jumped to about 75%. In our small community, most people have attended a visitation here and have seen firsthand how the Life Reflections shows work. Now when they come to arrange a funeral for a loved one, they show up for the arrangement conference with photos in hand. In fact, Life Reflections has transformed the arrangement conference itself. Now, instead of talking about details and filling out paperwork, we end up looking through the stack of photos and talking about the unique life of the person who died. It really makes for a much more personal, interactive arrangement conference."

Beacham adds that the Life Reflections shows also make wonderful, archival-quality keepsakes; he makes them available to families after the funeral for about $10 each. (That's where his CD burner comes in handy.) Anyone who has a PC running Windows can just click on the file he's created for them and it will run. It's as easy as that.

The Secular Service

When a family who hasn't darkened the door of a church in decades comes to you, you may not know how to help. They don't belong to a spiritual community; they're not interested in a religious service or any talk about God; they may be skeptical of the need for a funeral period. How do you create exceptional funeral experiences for these families?

Long-time funeral director Ray Rossell of Pray Funeral Home in Charlotte, Michigan has found a way. Thanks to the efforts of Rossell, Pray now offers a new, personalized and highly innovative style of funeral ceremony. They call it the Family Affirmation Service SM.

Rossell and a clergy friend got together and decided to develop an informal, participatory service based on the life of the deceased. After all, a life had been lived and it had impacted other people. "Most families see the value in honoring this if they are guided to talk about the life of the deceased," says Rossell.

The Family Affirmation Service often begins with a combination visitation/funeral service, which they call "a gathering of friends." The gathering takes place in a rather informal setting, such as the family's home or a favorite outdoor setting. They also hold Affirmation Services in their visitation room, but they rearrange furniture so the room looks more like a family room in your house. The body may or may not be present. A facilitator, sometimes a clergy member Rossell has helped select or sometimes a layperson the family has chosen, leads those gathered in sharing memories of the person who died. Often music is played and the family may sing a favorite hymn or song. Afterwards the family shares refreshments and talks informally among themselves. Typically the Family Affirmation Service concludes with a procession and committal service the following day at the burial site. Rossell often leads the brief service at the grave himself.

"We make a concerted effort to personalize both parts of the Affirmation Service as much as possible," says Rossell. "I try to make sure that all the important aspects of the life of the deceased are represented somehow, through music, sharing memories, choice of flowers, memorabilia displays, etc."

Rossell points out that in planning for this type of service, the initial family interview is critical. He sits down with the family and first asks them about the events that led to the death, since this is foremost in their minds. Then he begins to ask them about the life of the deceased.

"For at-need families, there is a tendency to measure the value of a person's life based on the last few weeks, rather than its entirety," Rossell says. "I try to lead the family back to the memories and life events the individual experienced. As the family remembers accomplishments, anecdotes and activities the deceased enjoyed, they begin to see the value in honoring the life somehow—even if they came to the interview prepared to request direct cremation."

If the family chooses to have a Family Affirmation Service, Rossell then helps them choose a facilitator and arranges to meet with the family and the facilitator within the next day, usually at the family's home. He has even created a workbook for this second planning session that helps him and the facilitator give structure to what might otherwise be a somewhat chaotic ceremony. They select an opening, music, often prayer or other readings and a closing to the ceremony. It's also important that the facilitator be prepared to lead the memory-sharing part of the service and know how to skillfully handle stretches of silence, guests who want to share unpleasant memories, etc.

Opening

A funeral's opening typically articulates the purpose for the event: John Smith has died and we have gathered together to remember his life and mourn his death. Though it may not be longer than a few sentences, the opening is important because it clearly marks the beginning of the funeral service and sets the tone for what is to follow.

Mourning need	Ways to meet this need	Your ideas
1. Acknowledge the the death.	Use the name of reality of the person who died. Depending on the circumstances, you might also mention how he or she died: "Many of you are aware that Mary has been ill with cancer over the past two years." Avoid euphemisms such as "expired."	
2. Move toward the pain of the loss.	Acknowledge the mourners' pain in your opening statements: "Blessed are they that mourn, for they shall be comforted" is appropriate for many people of faith.	
3. Remember the person who died.	Pause for a moment before beginning the ceremony's next segment to allow for reflection.	
4. Develop a new self-identity.	Acknowledge the interre latedness of all mourners in attendance: "Our unique relationships with John Smith and his family bring us here today . . . "	
5. Search for meaning.	Acknowledge the mourners' search for meaning in your opening statements. You might say, "Many of us are	

	asking why this has happened. . . "	
6. Receive support from others.	As you open, ask people to pause for a few moments and introduce themselves to those around them. This helps build mutual support. Thank everyone for coming and acknowledge their important roles in helping each other heal: "As Hillel said, 'Do not separate yourself from community'."	

Readings

Religious funeral ceremonies typically contain a number of standard readings from the faith's body of literature. Like secular ceremonies, they may also allow time for readings that in some way represent the person who died. I encourage personalized readings—not to the exclusion of the former but at least as a supplement.

Mourning need	Ways to meet this need	Your ideas
1. Acknowledge the reality of the death.	Consider readings that specifically mention that death has occurred. At the funeral we are in the midst of death and at least some of the readings should reflect this fact.	
2. Move toward the pain of the loss.	Choose at least one or two readings that in some way help mourners embrace their pain. Avoid using just uplifting, "he's gone to a better place" readings. As Kahlil Gibran wrote, "Your pain	

	is the breaking of the shell that encloses your understanding."	
3. Remember the person who died.	Help select readings that best capture unique life and philosophies of the person who died. Don't hesitate to inject some appropriate humor: "Bill told me just last month that he wanted his epitaph to read, 'I told you I was sick.'" Preface each of these personalized readings with a few words about the reading's place in the dead person's life: "Auden was Bill's favorite poet. This poem is from a book Bill gave to Sarah on their first wedding anniversary."	
4. Develop a new self-identity.	Involve people in attendance at the funeral in the readings. Ask a friend, a coworker, a family member, etc. to read a preselected piece or passage. (Remember they may need to have others standing with them as a means of support. Or, they may need you to be prepared to complete the reading if they are unable to.) Some may not want to read; for them a reading or a memory placed in the program may help them feel included.	

5. Search for meaning.	Appropriate readings are one of the most important funereal vehicles for the mourners' search for meaning. Religious and secular philosophical readings alike typically place the death in a larger context of meaning and thus offer comfort to mourners. Encourage family members to consider personalized readings: "John will now share with us a poem his mother wrote for him when he was just six years old." Remember, readers may need your help in practicing the reading aloud before the service. Help choose readings that reflect the individual family's context of meaning.	
6. Receive support from others.	In some support communities, it may be appropriate for you to encourage those attending the funeral to hold hands during the readings. Responsive readings can demonstrate group support. Leader: "The Lord is my shepherd; I shall not want." All: "He makes me lie down in green pastures and leads me beside still waters."	

Including Children in the Funeral

Most of the rituals in our society focus on children. What would birthdays or Christmas be without kids? Unfortunately, the funeral ritual, whose purpose is to help bereaved people begin to heal, is for many adults not seen as a ritual for kids. Too often, children are not included in the funeral because adults want to protect them. The funeral is painful, they reason, so I will shelter the children from this pain.

Yes, funerals can be very painful, but children have the same right and privilege to participate in them as adults do.

As a funeral facilitator, you can help appropriately include children by:

- **Helping parents explain the funeral to their children.**
  Unless they have attended one before, children don't know what to expect from a funeral. You can help by explaining what will happen before, during and after the ceremony. Give as many specifics as the child seems interested in hearing.

  If the body will be viewed either at a visitation or at the funeral itself, let the child know this in advance. Explain what the casket and the body will look like. If the body is to be cremated, explain what cremation means and what will happen to the ashes.

  You can also help children understand why we have funerals. Children need to know that the funeral is a time of sadness because someone has died, a time to honor the person who died, a time to help comfort and support each other and a time to affirm that life goes on.

- **Finding age-appropriate ways for children to take part in the funeral.**
  When appropriate, you might invite children to actually take part in the funeral. Bereaved children feel included when they can share a favorite memory or read a special poem as part of the funeral. Shyer children can participate by lighting a candle or placing something special (a memento, a drawing, a letter or a photo, for example) in the casket. And many children feel more included when they are invited simply to help plan the funeral service.

- **Understanding and accepting the child's way of mourning.**
  Help the family understand that children often need to accept their grief in doses, and that outward signs of grief may come and go. It is not unusual, for example, for children to want to roughhouse with their cousins during the visitation or play video games right after the funeral. Ask the parents to respect the child's need to be a child during this extraordinarily difficult time.

Music

As in many circumstances, music at the funeral helps set the mood. It is one way that we let people know that their emotions, which music tends to draw forth, are welcome at the funeral. Music is also a universal, unifying medium that joins mourners and speaks for them when words are inadequate.

Mourning need	Ways to meet this need	Your ideas
1. Acknowledge the reality of the death.	Quiet reflection during musical interludes often stimulates acknowledgment of the reality of the death, particularly when the chosen piece was a known favorite of the person who died: "One of Janet's favorite hymns was "Lift Up Your Hearts." As we join together in song, we realize she would smile with us while we embrace our memories of this faith-filled person."	
2. Move toward the pain of the loss.	Don't avoid music that helps people embrace their sadness. Music is often very moving to the bereaved and can provide an effective interlude for funeral attendees to think about their loss and embrace their pain.	
3. Remember the who died.	Encourage family person members to choose music that best represents or was meaningful to the person who died: "Wasn't your dad always walking around singing "Amazing Grace"? Would it be	

appropriate to include that hymn in the funeral?"

Print a few words in the program about each piece of music's meaning in the life of the dead person: "The song "Imagine" was one of Rachel's favorite's because. . ."

While music is being played, create an instant memory book by giving each participant a sheet of paper for jotting down a special memory of the person who died. Collect and bind the sheets at the end of the service. A grandchild might be asked to make the cover for the memory book.

4. Develop a new self-identity.

While an instrumental piece of music is being played, ask mourners to consider their own unique relationships with the person who died and how their lives will now change.

5. Search for meaning.

Though music is very individualistic and people often bring their own unique meanings to any given piece, certain pieces of music speak to a body of faith and often bring mourners meaning. For example, "How Great Thou Art" is a typical Christian hymn that helps mourners relate their loss to a broader context of meaning.

	At a more secular service I helped create, we used "The Circle of Life" from *The Lion King* and "In My Life" by the Beatles.	
	Have primary mourners light a candle while music is being played.	
6. Receive support from others.	Provide a time when music is being played for mourners to stand up and greet and comfort those around them.	

A Little Music Can Make a Big Difference

Michael Yobe of Poteet Funeral Home in Augusta, Georgia, tells us how he used personalized music on one occasion:

> *An elderly woman passed away when she was living in Texas, though she had been a longtime resident of Pittsburgh. It seems that Texas had quite an influence on her and she became fond of country music, Clint Black in particular. Upon her death, the family called me and we made the necessary arrangements to get her and them back to Pittsburgh for the viewing, funeral mass and burial.*
>
> *During the arrangement conference the family mentioned her fondness for Mr. Black. At the end of the meeting and acting on some unexplained impulse, I went to the local music store and purchased a CD containing her favorite song. Before the funeral mass, family and friends gathered at the funeral home for a prayer before going to church. At the conclusion of the prayer, I asked everyone to think of their fondest memories of the deceased while I played her favorite song. This was a total surprise to the family; there was not a dry eye in the place.*
>
> *I received many compliments about the personalized service at the committal. Weeks later (after the family discovered the CD with the registration book and flower cards), the family sent the best appreciation letter I ever received along with an invitation to fly to Texas to visit. They will never forget the funeral and I will never forget the feeling I had gotten by providing great service.*

Notice how Michael "acted on impulse." His gut and heart were telling him here was an opportunity to do something special, though not difficult, for a family. Listen to your gut. Follow your heart. Be a facilitator, not just a functionary.

The eulogy acknowledges the unique life of the person who died and affirms the significance of that life for all who shared in it. Without a eulogy and/or other personalized means of acknowledging this particular life and death, the funeral becomes an empty, cookie-cutter formality.

Mourning need	Ways to meet this need	Your ideas
1. Acknowledge the reality of the death.	Frequently use the name of the person who died.	
	Revisit the circumstances of the death.	
2. Move toward the pain of the loss.	Acknowledge the pain mourners are feeling.	
	Let mourners know that even if their faith embodies an afterlife, it is still necessary for them to mourn: "It has been said, 'At a time when one should be joyous, be joyous. And when it is time to mourn, mourn.' As we reflect on Jorge's life, we may remember happy times but we will also probably feel intense sadness."	
	If you, too, are a mourner in this funeral, model your own grief.	
3. Remember the person who died.	Done well, the eulogy can be the most memory-filled moment in the funeral. Write a meaningful eulogy by incorporating memories from many different people.	

Eulogy: To Bless

Let's remind ourselves that eulogy is a transliteration of the Greek word that means "to bless" or "to praise." The eulogy, or period of remembrance, is for saying good things about, or "blessing," the person who is being remembered.

I sometimes encounter clergy and others who believe that eulogies are somehow unnecessary, perhaps even bad. Some believe that eulogies takes the focus off God. I totally disagree. Remembering a life lived and being supported by faith are not mutually exclusive.

Distinguishing the obituary from the eulogy

It's also critically important to remember the distinction between an obituary and a eulogy. We have probably all been part of funerals where the officiant simply read the obituary but referred to it as a eulogy.

In contrast to the eulogy, the word obituary originates from the Latin word *obit*, which means departure. The obituary is usually a written declaration of a person's death. Facts outlined in the obituary usually include: the person's name; date and place of birth; date and place of death; place of employment; service club memberships; and names of survivors. As you know, some obituaries are more creative and interesting than others. However, simply reading the obituary is not a substitute for a meaningful eulogy or period of remembrance being integrated into the funeral service.

Some eulogy tips

Let's remind ourselves about some other important points surrounding eulogies:

- The eulogy may be delivered by a clergy person, a family member or a friend of the person who died. This person is called the "eulogist."
- Some non-faith families you serve may prefer to refer to this element of ceremony as "the period of remembrance." You should honor this request.
- Those who serve as eulogists are not always familiar with helpful guidelines in preparing a meaningful eulogy. You can help by drafting some guidelines for them.
- Instead of a traditional eulogy delivered by one person, several people can share memories during the eulogy time. Families often comment on how meaningful this has been to them. The families you serve today are teaching you that they want to be more involved than in the past. Historically, (and unfortunately, sometimes today) the funeral was all too often a passive experience for those in attendance. As we listen to families we find they often want the funeral to be as unique and personal as possible. A participant-oriented eulogy can help achieve this goal.

There is no right or wrong way to eulogize the person who died. If you help families to share memories and honor the person's life, you will have added more value to the funeral experience.

Using Symbols to Create a Meaningful Funeral Ceremony

As you work with bereaved families to plan authentic funeral ceremonies, help them understand and draw on the healing power of symbols.

In the funeral ritual, symbols such as the cross (for Christians; other faiths use other symbols), flowers and candles—and of course the dead person's body—provide points of focus for the bereaved. Because they represent such profound beliefs, they also tend to encourage the expression of painful thoughts and feelings. Furthermore, symbols such as these provide the comfort of tradition. Their continuity and timelessness grounds mourners at a time when all seems chaotic.

Symbolic acts, too, often enrich the grief-healing benefits of funerals. When mourners light a candle during the ceremony, for example, they are provided with a physical means of expressing their grief. Planting a memorial tree can be an emotional, physical and spiritual release; this act also creates a "point of mourning" for years to come.

The AIDS quilt and the Vietnam memorial wall are two beautiful, effective mourning symbols for all Americans. What small-scale, personalized symbols or symbolic acts might you be able to help bereaved families create before, during and after the funeral?

Below I have noted a few symbols often used in the context of the funeral ceremony. What others—traditional or untraditional—can you add?

Candle flames—spirit; also life's continuation even after death.

Cross—faith

Cup—nourishment, abundance, faith

Flowers—support, love, beauty

Mourning clothes—need for support, sadness

Water—source of life

____

____

____

____

____

____

	If you didn't know the person yourself, consider having someone else perform the eulogy.	
	Plan a less formal eulogy in which funeral participants are encouraged to stand up and share their most special memory of the person who died. (This may be greeted with some initial silence, but once someone speaks, this practice can be very moving and powerful.)	
4. Develop a new self-identity.	Speak directly to those whose self-identities will be most affected by the death: spouses or lovers, children, parents. Acknowledge their struggle to redefine themselves. Make an effort to include societally unacknowledged mourners, such as gay lovers, girlfriends/ boyfriends, divorced spouses. These "forgotten mourners" are in particular need of inclusion in the funeral process.	
5. Search for meaning.	Acknowledge the mourners' search for meaning. Speak to the meaning that the unique person who died brought to the lives of all he knew. Frame your comments about the meaning of this life and	

	this death in the context of the individual family's belief system: "During the holidays Betty and her family would read the poem "Crossing the Bar." Let's all join together in reading this poem."	
6. Receive support from others.	Tell those in attendance that their presence at the service speaks to the bereaved family at a time when words are inadequate.	

"Hope is not pretending that troubles don't exist…
It is the trust that they will not last forever,
That hurts will be healed and difficulties overcome…
It is faith that a source of strength and renewal
Lies within to lead us through the dark to the sunshine."
– Anonymous

Closing

Like the funeral's opening, the closing may be just a few words. But they are important words because they will likely leave a lasting impression on those in attendance.

Mourning need	Ways to meet this need	Your ideas
1. Acknowledge the reality of the death.	Sum up for mourners: "In bringing this service to a close we are symbolically acknowledging the ending of a life." Again, use the name of the person who died in your remarks.	
2. Move toward the pain of the loss.	Encourage the bereaved to embrace their pain in the weeks and months to come.	
3. Remember the person who died.	In your closing remarks, encourage mourners to silently reflect on the life of the person who died as they drive to the cemetery. Acknowledge that although the service is coming to a close, our relationship of memory with the person who died will continue on: "As we close, let's remember the words of Katie Brown McGowin who said, 'Little by little, step by step, I learned that I didn't need to hang on to the death to remember the life. What a joyous discovery.'"	

4. Develop a new self-identity.	Acknowledge the mourner's struggle for a new identity: "As we face the future without Lee, we acknowledge that we are forever changed by his death."	
5. Search for meaning.	Balance the embracing of pain with hope-filled, encouraging words. Close with an uplifting reading or song: "Let's close with a reading titled 'Hope.' Please join me."	
6. Receive support from others.	Encourage people to continue to support each other as they continue to journey through grief. Ask them to make a mental promise to phone or visit at least one other person in the room within the next week.	
	Let participants know what the immediate needs of the primary mourners are: "Joanne is unable to drive her car, so she will be needing some help getting groceries and running other errands."	

"Let us pray for ourselves, who are severely tested by death, that we do not try to minimize this loss or seek to escape from it, and also that we do not brood over it so that it overwhelms us and isolates us from others. May God grant us new courage and confidence to face life. Amen."

Committal

The burial of the body not only helps us acknowledge the reality and the finality of death, it also symbolizes the separation that the death has created. For these and other reasons described below, I encourage families to have committal services when at all possible and appropriate. It is also important to note that following cremation, some form of committal service is equally crucial. Whether the remains are to be buried, committed to a niche in a columbarium, scattered or even retained by the family, a ceremony marking this final stage in the funeral process is as necessary as the traditional committal.

Mourning need	Ways to meet this need	Your ideas
1. Acknowledge the reality of the death.	Create a service that includes the actual lowering of the casket into the ground. Have mourners throw handfuls of dirt into the gravesite. (Don't prescribe this but offer it to those who may find it meaningful.)	
2. Move toward the pain of the loss.	This may not be the most appropriate time during the ceremony for you to attempt to solicit the embracing of pain. Mourners will naturally confront their pain during the burial.	
3. Remember the person who died.	Select one brief, final reading that captures the life of the person who died. Observe a moment of silence in which each person thinks about their unique memories of the person who died: "Molly used to love to recite this	

	Irish Blessing. You may remember her words as she smiled and said . . . "	
4. Develop a new self-identity.	This need is often self-apparent, particularly as mourners walk away from the body in the burial spot.	
5. Search for meaning.	The committal is the funeral officiant's last opportunity to relate the death to a context of meaning. Because they are spoken last, your committal words may also be those that participants best remember: "As Don always said, 'Please remember me always for the love and the laughter.'"	
	Read a spiritual passage, quotation or poem that helps put the death into perspective for the family: "As we close, I ask you to join me in the 'Prayer for Those Who Mourn' . . ."	
6. Receive support from others.	Verbally invite everyone to attend the gathering and emphasize the importance of ongoing support. You might also print the invitation at the bottom of the service program.	
	Don't forget to include directions to the gathering's location.	

Gathering

Most funerals formally come to an end when the mourners gather to share a meal and to talk about the person who died. These gatherings often take place in a church meeting room, at a restaurant or at a home of a friend of family member. Like the visitation, the post-funeral gathering is an element of the funeral that facilitators don't often plan. Still, you might offer these suggestions to family members "in charge" of the gathering:

Mourning need	Ways to meet this need	Your ideas
1. Acknowledge the reality of the death.	The meaningful funeral will have fully dosed mourners with this reality by now. A natural "telling of the stories" of the person's life and death often take place, helping this need be met in doses.	
2. Move toward the pain of the loss.	Again, no conscious "pain-invoking" is necessary at this point. You might, however, educate the family about the importance of a gathering atmosphere that allows many different thoughts and feelings.	
3. Remember the person who died.	Designate a memory table on which friends and family members place items that capture the personality of the person who died and the unique relationships that person had. Photos, trophies, clothing and cherished belongings are all appropriate items for a memory table. (This may have already been done at the visitation.) The table then becomes a place for	

	mourners to visit and have private thoughts.	
	Some families are using this time to share a memory video of the person who died. This is where still photos (or possibly video footage) are edited together, often with music in the background, to create a montage of the person's life. Other families find a memory video too much work at this time, but may put one together and view it later on.	
4. Develop a new self-identity.	By encouraging families to have a gathering, you have helped them work on this mourning need.	
5. Search for meaning.	People will often talk in small groups at the gathering about their personal theories of life and death: "I figure that cancer is just one of God's ways of ending people's time on earth." Let the bereaved family know that this kind of discussion is valuable, but if other mourners are offering platitudes that seem unhelpful to them, they shouldn't take them to heart.	
6. Receive support from others.	The post-funeral gathering is a natural time for fellowship. At the gathering you might let the family know when you will be contacting them again.	

I have offered just a few suggestions for creating personalized, genuine funeral experiences. There are literally thousands of other ideas you might try as you help each individual family plan a funeral that will best meet their needs. Be creative and try not to be stifled by convention and formality. If your ideas help families meet the six reconciliation needs of mourning so that they can go on to find continued meaning in life and living—and in death—you will have done them a great service.

As gatekeepers of the death ritual, you are entrusted with a big responsibility. Helping people create meaningful funeral ceremonies, especially in this era of deritualization, is a daunting task. But it is also a critical one. I hope I have helped renew your commitment to every newly bereaved family in your care. Help them create meaningful funeral experiences and you will have helped society as a whole.

"Grief only becomes a tolerable and creative experience when love enables it to be shared with someone who really understands."
– Simon Stephens

Meaningful Funeral Experiences: An Outline

The following is provided as an outline for you to use as you design meaningful funeral experiences. You may want to photocopy it each time you plan a funeral. Do not let this outline limit your creativity, however; it is intended only as a springboard for your own ideas. You will probably need more writing room than this form provides, so you may want to attach blank sheets of paper or write on the backs of your photocopied pages.

Remember that the funeral is for survivors, and that meaningful funeral rituals help mourners embark on healthy grief journeys. Keep the reconciliation needs of mourning and the ways in which those needs can partially be met during the funeral firmly in mind as you complete this outline:

Need #1: Acknowledge the reality of the death

Need #2: Move toward the pain of the loss

Need #3: Remember the person who died

Need #4: Develop a new self-identity

Need #5: Search for meaning

Need #6: Receive ongoing support from others

Name of the person who died: ____________________________________.

Biographical information:____________________________________

____

____

____

Survivors (list family, friends and other relationships you will want to acknowledge or include during the service):

____

____

____

Attributes or passions of the person who died that we want to be sure to honor:

____

____

Memories to share

___

___

___

Person to lead the ceremony

___

Others who might want to speak or share memories

___

___

___

Honorary roles at the funeral:

Consider including those who loved the person who died by asking them to be a part of the ceremony.

Pallbearears (usually 6)

___

___

___

___

___

___

Honorary pallbearers___

Ushers___

Readers___

Singer/musicians___

Personal items that could be displayed (at the visitation, the service and/or the gathering afterwards): Photos, collections, hobby paraphernalia, artwork and many other objects that tangibly depict the life of the person who died are meaningful and appropriate to display.

____

____

____

____

Obituary

Special thoughts________________________________

____

____

To be reviewed by family__________________________

Submitted to____________________________________

Visitation

Public:

Date(s)______________________

Hours______________________

Private:

Date(s)______________________

Hours______________________

Personal Touches________________________________

____

____

____

The Funeral Ceremony

Date ________________ Place________________

Time________________

Officiant______________________

Officiant's phone number______________

Meeting with officiant____

Type of service____

Eulogy____

____

____

____

Music____

____

____

____

Symbols____

____

____

____

____

Other Personal Touches____

____

____

____

____

Committal Service

Cemetery____

Personal Touches____

____

____

____

Gathering

Place____

Personal Touches___________________________________

____

____

____

____

Special considerations

Here you may want to note the special considerations of this service. Are children among the primary mourners? How might they participate? Are there other mourners with special needs, e.g. a deaf person who might need someone to sign the service? Does the family want the service video- or audio-taped?

____

____

____

____

____

____

____

____

____

____

____

____

____

____

____

A Final Word

When someone we love dies, we must mourn if we are to fully love and live again. Yet, when the need to mourn is greatest, we seem most inclined to want to run away from it.

In this "mourning-avoiding" culture, more and more people appear to be running away from funerals. They are opting not to go through the doorway to their ultimate healing. As caregivers, we have both a responsibility and an opportunity to help our fellow human beings understand that to heal, they must mourn. And to mourn, they must have people around them who are understanding and supportive as they embrace the pain of their loss.

Meaningful funeral ceremonies provide us the forum to give testimony to the value we place on life. Funerals recognize that our love for someone has moved beyond the physical realm to the spiritual realm. What an opportunity and a privilege!

Yes, to experience and embrace the pain of loss is just as much a part of life as to experience the joy of love. The meaningful funeral ceremony provides a "safe place" were we can companion bereaved people as they fully enter into their grief.

We will be well-served to remember the powerful statement, "When words are inadequate, have a ritual." If we are able to "walk with" and be loving witnesses to people in their grief, chances are we can become a catalyst for a renewed sense of meaning and purpose in their continued lives.

Ten Freedoms for Creating Meaningful Funerals

(This list is written for bereaved families. Funeral facilitators may want to photocopy it and offer it as a handout as they work with families to plan the funeral.)

Meaningful funerals do not just happen. They are well-thought-out rituals that, at least for a day or two, demand your focus and your time. But the planning needn't be a burden if you keep in mind that the energy you expend now to create a personalized, inclusive ceremony will help you and other mourners in your grief journeys for years to come.

The following list is intended to empower you to create a funeral that will be meaningful to you and your family and friends. Remember—funerals are for the survivors.

1. *You have the right to make use of ritual.*
   The funeral ritual does more than acknowledge the death of someone loved. It helps provide you with the support of caring people. It is a way for you and others who loved the person who died to say, "We mourn this death and we need each other during this painful time." If others tell you that rituals such as these are silly or unnecessary, don't listen.

2. *You have the freedom to plan a funeral that will meet the unique needs of your family.*
   While you may find comfort and meaning in traditional funeral ceremonies, you also have the right to create a ceremony that reflects the unique personality of your family and the person who died. Do not be afraid to add personal touches to even traditional funerals.

3. *You have the freedom to ask friends and family members to be involved in the funeral.*
   For many, funerals are most meaningful when they involve a variety of people who loved the person who died. You might ask others to give a reading, deliver the eulogy, play music or even help plan the funeral.

4. *You have the freedom to view the body before and during the funeral.*
   While viewing the body is not appropriate for all cultures and faiths, many people find it helps them acknowledge the reality of the death. It also provides a way to say goodbye to the person who died. There are many benefits to viewings and open casket ceremonies; don't let others tell you this practice is morbid or wrong.

5. *You have the freedom to embrace your pain during the funeral.*
The funeral may be one of the most painful but also the most cathartic moments of your life. Allow yourself to embrace your pain and to express it openly. Do not be ashamed to cry. Find listeners who will accept your feelings no matter what they are.

6. *You have the freedom to plan a funeral that will reflect your spirituality.*
If faith is a part of your life, the funeral is an ideal time for you to uphold and find comfort in that faith. Those with more secular spiritual orientations also have the freedom to plan a ceremony that meets their needs.

7. *You have the freedom to search for meaning before, during and after the funeral.*
When someone loved dies, you may find yourself questioning your faith and the very meaning of life and death. This is natural and in no way wrong. Don't let others dismiss your search for meaning with clichéd responses such as, "It was God's will" or "Think of what you still have to be thankful for."

8. *You have the freedom to make use of memory during the funeral.*
Memories are one of the best legacies that exist after the death of someone loved. You will always remember. Ask your funeral officiant to include memories from many different people in the eulogy. Use a memory board or a memory table. Ask those attending the funeral to share their most special memory of the person who died with you.

9. *You have the freedom to be tolerant of your physical and emotional limits.*
Especially in the days immediately following the death, your feelings of loss and sadness will probably leave you feeling fatigued. Respect what your body and mind are telling you. Get daily rest. Eat balanced meals.

10. *You have the freedom to move toward your grief and heal.*
While the funeral is an event, your grief is not. Reconciling your grief will not happen quickly. Be patient and tolerant with yourself and avoid people who are impatient and intolerant with you, before, during and after the funeral. Neither you nor those around you must forget that the death of someone loved changes your life forever.

We Hope to Hear from You!

I would like to hear from you about the contents of *Creating Meaningful Funeral Experiences*. My writing plans include future revisions of this text and I would like to incorporate your comments—especially additional creative, practical ideas for the design and execution of meaningful funeral ceremonies.

Please write to me at the following address:

Alan D. Wolfelt, Ph.D.

The Center for Loss and Life Transition

3735 Broken Bow Road

Fort Collins, CO 80526

(970) 226-6050

drwolfelt@centerforloss.com

Sponsor or attend a workshop led by Dr. Wolfelt!

In addition to his writing and counseling, Dr. Wolfelt presents workshops across North America on bereavement-related topics—including creating meaningful funeral ceremonies. He also conducts seminars for bereavement caregivers at his Center for Loss and Life Transition in Fort Collins, Colorado. Please call or write him at the address above for more information, or visit his website: www.centerforloss.com.

About the Author

Dr. Alan Wolfelt is a noted author, educator and grief counselor. Recipient of the Association for Death Education and Counseling's Death Educator Award, he serves as Director of the Center for Loss and Life Transition in Fort Collins, Colorado and is on the faculty at the University of Colorado Medical School in the Department of Family Medicine.

Dr. Wolfelt is known internationally for his work in the areas of adult and childhood grief. Among his many other publications are the books *Understanding Your Grief: Ten Essential Touchstones for Finding Hope and Healing Your Heart, The Journey Through Grief, The Mourner's Book of Hope* and *Creating Meaningful Funeral Ceremonies: A Guide for Families*.

CPSIA information can be obtained at www.ICGtesting.com
Printed in the USA
LVOW10s1948190913

353066LV00003B/6/P